TRAIL GUIDE TO
GRAND STAIRCASE
ESCALANTE
NATIONAL MONUMENT

TRAIL GUIDE
TO
GRAND STAIRCASE
ESCALANTE
NATIONAL MONUMENT

David Urmann

GIBBS·SMITH
P
PUBLISHER

SALT LAKE CITY

First Edition
03 02 01 00 99   5 4 3 2 1

Published by
Gibbs Smith, Publisher
P.O. Box 667
Layton, Utah 84041

Orders: (1-800) 748-5439
Web site: *www.gibbs-smith.com*

Edited by Suzanne Taylor
Book design and production by J. Scott Knudsen, Park City, Utah
Printed and bound in the United States

Library of Congress Cataloguing-in-Publication Data
Urmann, David, 1974–
Trail guide to Grand Staircase–Escalante National
Monument/David Urmann.
p. cm.

ISBN 0-87905-885-4
1. Hiking—Utah—Grand Staircase–Escalante National
Monument—Guidebooks. 2. Trails—Utah—Grand
Staircase–Escalante National Monument—Guidebooks. 3. Grand
Staircase–Escalante National Monument (Utah)—Guidebooks.
I. Title.
GV199.42.U82G738 1999
917.92'51 dc21
                              98-31576
                              CIP

How to Use This Guide

A t 1.7 million acres, the Grand Staircase–Escalante National Monument is almost as large as Yellowstone National Park. It is crossed by only one paved road (Highway 12), and most of the sites and attractions are along gravel roads or four-wheel-drive routes. It is helpful to think of the monument in terms of three general areas: the Canyons of the Escalante, the Kaiparowits Plateau, and the Grand Staircase. Each area has unique features and characteristics. However, if you only have a short time to explore the monument, it is best to stay in one area, since driving on the long dirt roads that traverse the monument is time-consuming.

This guide begins with general background knowledge about the monument. The rest of the guide is divided into sections dealing with each area. Each section contains general information about the area and details its main access roads. Road descriptions are followed by a number of more detailed descriptions of hikes, camping areas, and other attractions found along the road.

The descriptions of hikes, campgrounds, and Indian ruins are assigned numbers. These numbers correspond to the numbers assigned to the maps in the book and also create an easy way to cross-reference material. For example, if a certain canyon or gulch is followed by a number in parentheses, it means that more detailed information about the subject can be found elsewhere in the guide.

This guide is designed for both the drive-through traveler and the person who may already be somewhat familiar with the monument. Some of my favorite hikes are listed on the next page. Hopefully, this will help people with time constraints sort through all the monument's possibilities.

Dave's Best Hikes and Drives in the
Grand Staircase–Escalante National Monument

Canyons of the Escalante

Hikes: Phipps Wash, the Lower Gulch, Lower Calf Creek

Drives: Highway 12 (Boulder to Escalante)

Other: Escalante River Crossing pictographs, Escalante Petrified
Forest State Park

Kaiparowits Plateau

Hikes: Dry Fork of Coyote Gulch, Trap Canyon

Drives: Smoky Mountain Road (Big Water to the top of Smoky
Mountain), Smoky Mountain Road (Alvey Wash)

Other: Grosvenor Arch, Smoky Mountain Burning Coal Beds

Grand Staircase

Hikes: Hackberry Canyon, the Paria River, Cottonwood Wash
Narrows

Drives: Cottonwood Wash Road

Other: Old Paria Movie Set, Cockscomb Overlook

1

Round Valley Draw

Background Information

Travel Guidelines and Information

O f all the national parks and monuments in the United States, Grand Staircase–Escalante National Monument is the only one where a high-clearance four-wheel drive is essential for exploring large areas of the backcountry. The monument's large size and numerous physical barriers—such as rough roads, giant cliffs, and deep canyons—make travel within the monument move at a slower pace than most are used to. For example, it takes over five hours to drive the seventy-eight-mile length of Smoky Mountain Road. The remoteness and isolation of the monument are two of its most appealing features, but these same qualities can cause trouble for the unprepared traveler. Traveling safely means being prepared and informed.

No services are available within the monument, so plans must be made to refuel and resupply in surrounding towns. The principal access roads into the monument are unpaved except for the Burr Trail and Highway 12, and road conditions vary dramatically with weather changes. Bad weather can leave any of the unpaved roads impassable for days or weeks, especially in winter when dirt roads are not plowed or maintained.

Travelers planning to leave the main roads described in this book should carefully prepare themselves. Even some of the described roads, such as Croton Road, are quite rough and little traveled. I spent two days driving the seventy or so miles of Croton Road, eight hours' driving time, and did not see a single person. Those planning extensive travel on long rough roads should bring at least the supplies that follow:

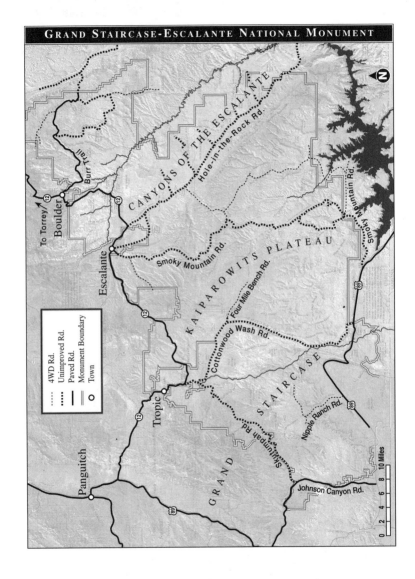

GRAND STAIRCASE-ESCALANTE NATIONAL MONUMENT

CANYONS OF THE ESCALANTE

Hole-in-the-Rock Rd.

Burr Trail

To Torrey 12

Boulder

Escalante

Smoky Mountain Rd.

KAIPAROWITS PLATEAU

Smoky Mountain Rd.

Four Mile Bench Rd.

Cottonwood Wash Rd.

89

4WD Rd.
Unimproved Rd.
Paved Rd.
Monument Boundary
Town

Tropic

G R A N D   S T A I R C A S E

Nipple Ranch Rd.

89

Skutumpah Rd.

Panguitch

Johnson Canyon Rd.

89

0   2   4   6   8   10 Miles

1. **Gasoline:** Always start trips into the monument with a full tank of gas. I always carry a five-gallon jerry can of gas in my vehicle and have used it numerous times.

2. **Water:** For any trip it is wise to bring at least five gallons of water in your vehicle. When hiking in hot weather, plan on drinking at least a gallon a day.

3. **Food, clothing, and a first-aid kit**.

4. **Maps:** Many of the secondary roads are not marked by signs, so maps are essential.

5. **Cellular phone:** It is possible to use a cellular phone at a few places in the monument. Consider bringing one during the off-season or if you are traveling alone.

6. **Vehicle parts:** Bring the basic tools and a good spare tire.

7. **Chains:** Chains might be helpful in winter when the roads are slick and icy. Chains will do a lot more to improve your traction than a four-wheel-drive vehicle can.

Flash Floods: Flash floods are serious. Imagine a wall of water rushing down a narrow canyon, carrying boulders the size of cars. In 1977, eleven people hiking in Antelope Canyon, just outside the monument's boundaries, died because they did not take the threat of flash floods seriously. Hikers should avoid hiking in washes during periods of thunderstorm activity. The rain from the thunderstorm that generated the flood in Antelope Canyon fell eleven miles upstream from the hikers.

Thunderstorms can build rapidly during afternoon heat. The sky can go from being perfectly clear to being dark and threatening in a matter of hours. When hiking in a narrow canyon, it is often difficult to get a clear and unobstructed view of the sky. As a result, clouds and thunderstorms may develop that cannot be seen from the confines of a narrow canyon. If thunderstorms or building cumulus clouds are seen anywhere in the area, there is the potential for flash flooding. Check forecasts and know what kind of weather patterns result in flash floods.

Flash floods occur most often during the summer months as a result of thunderstorm activity, but strong, organized storm systems can generate flash floods at any time during the year. Prolonged and especially heavy rain can trigger flash floods. One last word of advice: never camp in or close to a dry wash.

Four-Wheel-Drive Roads: Much of the monument can only be explored by four-wheel-drive routes. These roads are unmaintained, rocky, rutted, sandy, seldom traveled, and easy to get stuck on. Knowing your vehicle's capabilities, and using a little common sense, will keep you out of trouble. A fine line exists between adventure and danger.

Always watch the weather. If weather conditions are deteriorating, return to a good road. Bad weather can leave dirt roads, especially clay roads, impassable for days. Many routes can be descended but are more difficult to ascend. This is always the case with thick sand.

Lowering tire pressure can help you get out of sandy areas. However, if you need to lower the pressure in your tires, immediately reinflate them. Driving long distances with underinflated tires may cause them to lose their bead and can cause sidewall flex, resulting in tire failure.

It is illegal to travel off the monument's existing roadways. In response to off-road landscape damage, the Bureau of Land Management (BLM) will probably close many of the four-wheel-drive routes that now exist. To avoid further closures of four-wheel-drive routes, we all need to adhere to a "Tread Lightly" ethic.

Weather in the Monument

Because the monument is a large area, its wide elevation ranges allow for large weather differences from place to place. The southern part of the monument near Kanab averages about ten degrees warmer throughout the year than the Boulder-Escalante area. But at a lower elevation, Kanab receives slightly more yearly rainfall than

Boulder—thirteen inches as opposed to ten inches. In general, the wettest periods are during the winter and late summer.

Spring: The weather in the spring is highly variable. It is quite possible that one day will be cold and windy (temperatures in the 50s), while the following day will be warm and sunny (temperatures in the 70s to 80s). Organized storm systems occasionally come in off the coast, but the weather is generally good. Spring is one of the best times to visit the monument. Leaves come out on the cottonwood trees in April and spring wildflowers bloom.

Summer: Most days are clear and hot (90s to 100s). Monsoonal moisture from Arizona periodically travels north into Utah and causes summer thunderstorms. Thunderstorm season is in full force from mid-July through August. Due to the threat of flash floods during this period, hikers should obtain daily weather forecasts before hiking in slot canyons. The narrow shaded canyons, which offer a respite from the summer heat, are also the same canyons most at risk for a flash flood on a hot day.

Fall: Fall usually has the best weather. Thunderstorms occur into September, but October is usually a tranquil month with clear skies. The leaves on the cottonwood and aspen trees begin changing colors, first the aspen at higher elevations and then the cottonwoods during October and November. The first winter storms usually come in November, bringing snow to the higher elevations.

Winter: Most roads in the monument are inaccessible, but conditions vary depending on storm frequency and amount of snowfall. The weather is generally clear and cold, but be prepared for snowstorms. Temperatures are below freezing at night and generally rise into the 40s during the day. Cold water makes stream crossings miserable, and short days seem even shorter in narrow dark canyons. Hiking can be difficult as ice builds up in canyons that normally contain running water. Few other visitors are seen during the winter months. One of my favorite aspects of winter is that the sun's low angle creates subtle lighting for most of the day, which is very favorable to photography.

TOWNS AND SERVICES

Highway 12

Torrey

Torrey is the gateway to Capitol Reef National Park and lies thirty-five miles north of the monument's boundaries. Motels are available most of the time on a twenty-four-hour basis. The gas stations in town close around 11 P.M., and the town is host to a small general store and a few cafes.

Boulder

Boulder consists of a few motels, gas stations, and a cafe. Services in Boulder close at night and some may be closed on Sundays.

Escalante

The town of Escalante has a twenty-four-hour gas station and motels. The grocery store, auto service station, and BLM ranger station are open during the day, and a bank with an ATM is found on the west side of town. After a long day on the trail, Escalante offers some good places to eat.

Henrieville & Cannonville

There are currently no services available in these towns; however, this could change as the monument becomes better traveled. It appears that a gas station/motel is already being built in Cannonville.

Tropic

This small town is mainly oriented toward the tourist. The gas station/motel in the middle of town has a good supply of groceries. A few other motels and restaurants are also located in Tropic. The availability of services in Tropic is subject to the time of year, and no services are available on a twenty-four-hour basis.

Highway 89

Panguitch

Panguitch is the gateway to Bryce Canyon National Park. It is a full-service town with accommodations and gas available on a twenty-four-hour basis. The grocery store, hardware store, and ranger station keep regular business hours.

Kanab

Kanab is the largest town in the area of the monument. As a result, it is a good place to get supplies and stay the night. This town is large enough to support some large twenty-four-hour grocery stores. The BLM office is a good place to get maps and information.

Big Water

Big Water consists of a small convenience store without gasoline services.

Greene

Greene is located on the Utah/Arizona border, six miles east of Big Water. It has a gas station that is open year-round.

Page

Located seventy-five miles east of Kanab, Page is a large town with all services available. Page sits on the shores of Lake Powell, adjacent to the Glen Canyon Dam.

The Anasazi and Fremont

Stumbling onto ancient ruins or rock-art sites is one of the most exciting prospects of hiking the monument. Its abundant ruins and rock art make archeology accessible to all of us. The monument is one of the few places where the Anasazi and Fremont cultures overlapped and interacted, so a wide variety of architectural and rock-art styles exists.

The history of Native Americans begins about 8,000 years ago, long before the time of the Anasazi and Fremont. These ancient hunter-gatherers lived in small clans and, since they had no form of agriculture, led a purely nomadic existence looking for wild plants.

It was not until about 2,500 years ago that these tribes began to develop simple systems of agriculture. Perhaps they supplemented their diet by planting a few crops in the spring and harvesting them in the fall. The granaries, hidden high on the canyon walls, could have been used to store seed so that these nomadic farmers would have enough to plant another crop.

As agricultural methods improved, the tribes gradually became more dependent on farming and were able to settle down and live in one place. Settling down allowed these people to build dwellings in which to live and store goods. Most of the rock art and ruins were created during this stage of cultural progression, between 800 and 1,200 years ago. Archeologists consider this time period to be the stage of maximum cultural progression of both the Anasazi and Fremont.

Prehistoric cultures are grouped by the types of artifacts they leave behind. The Fremont differed from the Anasazi in that they did not build kivas, they made sandals out of animal hide rather than yucca plants, and their pottery and baskets were less advanced. The rock-art figures of the Fremont are typically trapezoidal-shaped, elaborately dressed human figures, while those of the Anasazi are more varied.

The Anasazi, generally considered more advanced than the Fremont, dominated an area to the east and south of the Colorado River, and the Fremont lived to the north and west of the Colorado River.

The Fremont Indians are named after the Fremont River, which runs through Capitol Reef. Fremont ruins are found over a broad area ranging from the shores of the Great Salt Lake, to the Uinta Basin, to Capitol Reef National Park. The landscape in this wide area varies from the well-watered high plateaus of central Utah to the barren salt flats and playas of the Great Salt Lake Desert.

The Fremont were probably as diverse a people as the landscape in which they lived. Individual tribes might have spoken different languages and had different religious beliefs. Some may have continued nomadic lifestyles, while others profited by settling down and growing crops. The numerous lifestyles of the Fremont make classification difficult, and artifacts at one site are difficult to compare to those of another. Nevertheless, some type of contact must have occurred at times between these various bands of Fremont, as all archeological sites share a few key artifacts.

The Anasazi built the giant ruins at Navajo National Monument, Canyon de Chelly, Hovenweep, and Chaco Canyon. They are well known for the intricate designs of their buildings, religious kivas, and even road systems. The Fremont ruins never obtained the complexity displayed by Anasazi ruins, and in this sense the Fremont are considered less advanced than the Anasazi.

Many of the Fremont and Anasazi advancements were adapted from Mexico's more-developed cultures. Mexico's cultural advancements gradually spread north over hundreds of years, first to the Anasazi and then later to the Fremont.

The monument represents a transitional zone between the Fremont and Anasazi, and many of the archeological sites show traits of both cultures. An easily seen example of this is the large Fremont-style petroglyphs in Calf Creek Canyon (3) and the nearby presence of a kiva at the Coombs Site in Anasazi State Park (1).

The absence of ruin and storage sites and the change to more primitive rock-art types are signs of the disappearance of the Fremont and Anasazi. This occurred around 750 years ago, and evidence shows that the Anasazi culture moved south and that the Fremont culture completely vanished.

Explanations for this abrupt disappearance include climate change and invasion, with eventual cultural assimilation by less-advanced hunter-gatherer tribes. Tree-ring evidence suggests some type of climate change, but it is unknown if this climate change was a large-enough factor to destroy the culture. Did successive crop failures cause a breakdown of societal structure, or did nomadic tribes invade the area? The answer may be a combination of both.

Many of the ways the Fremont and Anasazi lived remain a mystery, like what religious beliefs they had, and how they related to this world of stone and rock. What we do know is that they lived within the monument, grew crops, and struggled daily to exist. Their ancient stone ruins and faded pictographs capture the imagination and take us back at least one step into the past.

ROCK ART

Rock art can be subdivided into two different types: petroglyphs and pictographs. Petroglyphs are made by chipping or carving rock from flat surfaces. Pictographs are made by applying colored pigments to rock surfaces.

One of the monument's characteristic features is the number of different styles of petroglyphs and pictographs. The various styles are attributed to the Fremont and Anasazi and to other nomadic peoples who lived within the monument. Rock art captures our attention and invites speculation on why it was created. Interpreting rock art is difficult and has often been ignored by the professional archeologist, who has focused more on the ancient ruins and dwellings of these prehistoric cultures.

The best surfaces for rock art are uniform in texture and display flat vertical faces. Rock art is rarely found on horizontal planes. The presence of a dark coat of desert varnish was also desirable, as less work was required to create a high-contrast image. Rock art is found not only on canyon walls and cliffs but also on the large flat surfaces of boulders that litter the talus and canyon bottoms.

Rock-art sites are concentrated in certain areas, although suitable rocks exist almost everywhere. Rock art is most likely found near canyons with flowing water, places that have other signs of Indian occupation such as ruins, or near landmarks such as the confluence of two canyons. Pictographs are found in the same types of locations as petroglyphs, but also need to be sheltered from the elements. If the pigments used to create a pictograph were exposed to rain and wind, they would have been quickly washed away. Pictographs are commonly found in large alcoves and under rock overhangs, which protect them from the elements.

The subject matter of rock art is quite varied. Human figures and animals are often displayed. The most likely animals appear to be bighorn sheep and deer. Humans are often displayed as being elaborately dressed or just as simple stick figures. Often rock art is non-representational and abstract, composed of wavy lines, dots, concentric circles, and other geometric shapes.

Rock art was probably created for a number of reasons. It could have been to mark territorial boundaries or game trails and travel routes. Some panels were probably created for ceremonial and religious purposes, while other panels could have been used as astronomical calendars. Very few sites focus on female activities such as growing crops, making pottery, or building shelters. Most archeologists believe rock art was created primarily by males because most of the sites feature such traditional male activities as hunting and religion.

Many of the old-timers of Escalante and Boulder were the first collectors of Indian artifacts. Most of the significant artifacts were donated to Edison Alvey, who ran a small museum in the town of Escalante. The museum had an amazing collection of pottery and arrowheads, but the museum was robbed and burned in the 1980s, and irreplaceable treasures were lost.

Most archeologists and hikers feel protective of rock-art sites to the point of keeping their locations secret. Many of the small-town locals know of at least one site, and they may be willing to tell you how to get there; but for the most part, you will have to explore and find them on your own.

Geology of the Monument

The Grand Staircase–Escalante National Monument is part of the larger region of the Colorado Plateau. The Colorado Plateau is an arid land except for a few high mountains that capture the winter snows, and it is this desert atmosphere that makes the plateau a land of cliffs and canyons. If the Colorado Plateau received more rain, plants would grow, soils would form, and the sharp profiles of the cliffs and canyons would take on a more subdued appearance.

The Colorado Plateau is characterized by visible and continuous layers of sedimentary rocks. The sedimentary rocks were deposited as layers of sediment in lakes and oceans, and on land by wind and water. Sedimentary rocks preserve clues to the environment in which they were deposited, such as fossils, ripple marks, mud cracks, and cross-bedding. The oldest layers of sediment are buried the deepest so the youngest are near the top. Geologists group multiple layers of sediment that were deposited in the same environment during a specific time period into formations.

The entire area of the Colorado Plateau has been uplifted to expose the sedimentary rocks that were once deeply buried. The rocks of the plateau have been altered little by geologic forces and, for the most part, remain in the same horizontal position in which they were deposited. It is these relatively flat layers that give rise to the flat-topped mesas and plateaus that are such a dominant part of the Colorado Plateau scenery.

THE GRAND STAIRCASE

The Grand Staircase is literally a giant staircase of plateaus and cliffs that rises 7,000 feet in the eighty miles between the Grand Canyon and the rim of Bryce Canyon. The sedimentary rocks beautifully displayed in the Grand Staircase offer a unique look into the earth's past. Nowhere else in the Colorado Plateau is such a geologically intact display of sedimentary rocks found. From the bottom of the Grand Canyon, where the oldest rocks are exposed, to the rim of Bryce Canyon, where the youngest rocks are exposed, the rocks tell of two billion years of the earth's history.

Beginning at the bottom of the Grand Staircase, the Kaibab Limestone forms a broad plateau stretching from the rim of the Grand Canyon to the first set of cliffs of the Grand Staircase. The Kaibab Limestone is the oldest rock formation exposed within the monument. It contains fossil seashells and corals that were deposited in an ocean 250 million years ago. The limestone is named after Kaibab Gulch, a deep, steep-walled gorge in the monument where the limestone is well exposed (*see* Kaibab Gulch on page 135).

The Chocolate Cliffs are the first step of cliffs and are made up of the more-resistant Shinarump Conglomerate and the less-resistant Moenkopi Formation (*see* How Do Cliffs Form? on page 23). The Moenkopi is a reddish-brown mudstone that forms the cliff base. This formation was deposited on a broad coastal plain that formed as the ancient seas retreated westward. The rocks of the Moenkopi

Formation preserve numerous tracks of ancient reptiles and amphibians as well as ripple marks and the casts of mud cracks.

The Vermilion Cliffs rise above the Chocolate Cliffs. These cliffs are made up of the less-resistant Chinle Formation and the more-resistant Wingate Sandstone. The best place to see the Vermilion Cliffs is along Highway 89 between Kanab and Page. Members of the Powell Survey of 1871 named the cliffs for their striking colors.

HOW DO CLIFFS FORM?

Cliffs are a prominent part of southwestern landscape. They often run for miles and can be of great height like the cliffs of the Grand Staircase. Cliff formation is a result of harder, more-resistant rocks overlying weaker, less-resistant rocks.

Less-resistant rocks are more easily eroded than stronger rocks. If the stronger rocks are sitting on top of the weaker rocks, the result is that the stronger rocks are slowly undermined as the less-resistant rocks erode more quickly. The correct combination of sedimentary formations is very important for cliff formation.

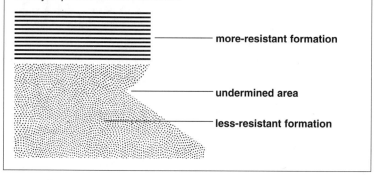

The Chinle Formation forms the multicolored base of the Vermilion Cliffs. The Chinle is the same formation in which the petrified wood at the Petrified Forest National Park in Arizona is preserved. It was deposited in a large continental basin, and signs of ancient stream channels and lake beds are preserved in the rock. Minerals from volcanic ash layers in the rock are responsible for the formation's wide color variety. The Painted Desert on the Navajo Indian Reservation in Arizona is made up of the Chinle Formation.

Within the Grand Staircase–Escalante National Monument, the Chinle Formation is best exposed near the Old Paria Movie Set (41) and along Wolverine Road (13), which is the best location to see petrified wood in the Chinle.

The steep walls of the Vermilion Cliffs are made of Wingate Sandstone, which forms many of the large red cliffs of southern Utah, including those seen in Capitol Reef National Park and Canyonlands National Park. Within the monument, Wingate forms the escarpments of the Circle Cliffs, which are visible from the Burr Trail.

Wingate Sandstone was deposited in a desert environment and, as a result, displays cross-bedding. Cross-bedding is a result of sand dunes migrating across the ancient desert. Cross-beds are sedimentary layers deposited at an

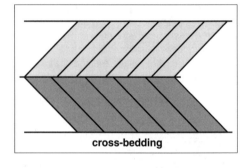

cross-bedding

angle to the layers below, the result of deposition by wind or a moving current rather than a slow settling as in a lake (see cross-bedding graphic above).

The Kayenta Formation forms a series of small benches and terraces between the Vermilion Cliffs and the next set of cliffs above them, the White Cliffs. The Kayenta Formation is made up of multiple layers of more-resistant sandstones that form ledges and small cliffs and less-resistant shales that form benches and terraces. The Kayenta was deposited in stream channels and floodplains during a brief period when the giant deserts, represented by the Wingate and Navajo Sandstones, became more hospitable.

The White Cliffs are made of the well-known Navajo Sandstone, which is a dominant rock in southern Utah. Many of the canyons of the upper Paria River and the Escalante River are cut into this rock. It is also the same sandstone that forms Zion Canyon in Zion National Park. The best views of the White Cliffs are from Nipple

Ranch Road (*see* description on page 144) and from the top of the Cockscomb (37). Navajo Sandstone tends to weather into large rounded-stone monoliths, and the best slot canyons in the monument cut into the Navajo Sandstone. The Navajo, like the Wingate, was deposited by migrating sand dunes in a giant desert and is cross-bedded. The desert in which the Wingate and Navajo Sandstone was deposited has been compared by geologists to the modern-day Sahara Desert both in size and aridity.

Entrada Sandstone lies above the top of the White Cliffs and tends to weather into beautiful and alluring shapes. The best exposures of Entrada Sandstone are in the vicinity of Kodachrome Basin State Park (31). The deep-red colors and soft, smooth textures make this a beautiful rock. Entrada Sandstone is the same formation that forms the stone monoliths of Cathedral Valley at Capitol Reef and twisted rock forms of Goblin Valley State Park.

The Gray Cliffs lie above the White Cliffs and visually do not stand out nearly as well. The rocks of the Gray Cliffs were deposited in a large ocean about ninety million years ago. The appearance of this ocean marks the end of the period of great deserts, represented by Wingate and Navajo Sandstone.

For the most part, the Gray Cliffs are composed of Tropic shale, which is named after the town of Tropic where it is most visible and easily identified. Besides the town of Tropic, the best place to see Tropic shale is in the area of desolate badlands called "The Blues" (30), located about fifteen miles east of Tropic along Highway 12. Tropic shale is an excellent formation in which to look for marine fossils, as it contains large oyster beds, mollusks, shark teeth, and ammonites.

The often-overlooked Brown Cliffs are above the Gray Cliffs and are composed of the Straight Cliff Formation and Wahweap Sandstone, the dominant rocks of the Kaiparowits Plateau. The Straight Cliffs Formation is named after the Straight Cliffs, which form the eastern edge of the Kaiparowits Plateau. The Wahweap and Straight Cliff Formations were deposited on a broad coastal plain dominated by lagoons and swamps around sixty million years ago. This large low-lying coastal area formed as the ocean that deposited the Tropic shale gradually retreated. It was in these antiquated swamps and floodplains that the great coal deposits of the Kaiparowits Plateau were laid down.

The Pink Cliffs, above the Gray Cliffs, make up the scenic formations of Bryce Canyon National Park and Table Mountain along the northern and eastern boundaries of the monument. These rocks were deposited quite recently, geologically speaking, in a large freshwater lake.

History and Settlement

EXPLORATION AND DISCOVERY OF THE U.S.'S LAST UNMAPPED REGION

In 1870, John Wesley Powell, the first man to successfully navigate the Colorado River, began making plans for a second trip down the river to complete the topographical surveys he began on his first voyage in 1869. Jacob Hamblin, a seasoned Mormon explorer, was put in charge of setting up a supply point for the expedition at the junction of the Dirty Devil and Colorado Rivers.

Using maps of the region made by Powell on his first journey down the Colorado, Hamblin planned to take the extra supplies from Kanab to the mouth of the Dirty Devil River by means of an overland route. Hamblin accidentally discovered the Escalante River when he mistook it for the Dirty Devil. In doing so, he became the first white man to travel down the Escalante River Canyon as he tried to carry Powell's supply goods to the mouth of what he thought was the Dirty Devil River. The blame for this mistake cannot be placed entirely on Hamblin, as he was using maps made by Powell, who had not noticed the Escalante River on his first trip down the Colorado.

The Almon Thompson-Fredric Dellenbaugh party, under the direction of Powell in 1872, officially discovered the Escalante River. Almon Thompson continued to explore and map the region between 1872 and 1875. Many of the regional place-names were given by Thompson and other members of various Powell expeditions: Kaiparowits Plateau, Escalante and Dirty Devil Rivers, Henry Mountains, Vermilion Cliffs, and Aquarius Plateau. Thompson also advised the early Mormon settlers to name their settlement "Escalante" after the Spanish explorer who crossed the Colorado River in the 1700s.

SETTLEMENT

The Escalante valley was settled by Mormons in spring 1875. Many of the original settlers had struggled across the plains with the Mormons on their journey to the Great Salt Lake Valley in the late 1840s and had lived there long enough to become established and prosperous before they were called upon by the Mormon Church to help settle southern Utah. However, Escalante was not settled as a result of orders given by the Mormon Church. Rather, the first settlers of Escalante moved there from Panguitch, hoping that the lower elevation of the Escalante River Valley offered a climate that would be better suited for agriculture.

The early settlers of Escalante had to overcome and deal with many hardships. The first year, the settlers lived in dugouts, cellars dug into the ground with roofs of poles and willows. The men of the community were too busy building irrigation systems and planting crops to build houses. Everything was done by hand in the settlement for the first couple of years. Deer meat was preserved, grain was threshed and ground, and candles and soap were made from animal by-products. Imagine living under these conditions while taking into account that the average family who settled in Escalante included four or five children when it first moved there, a number that would later increase to thirteen or fourteen.

In the years before World War II, the Navajos used to cross the Colorado River and come to the town of Escalante to trade. Typically, the Navajos would trade their handwoven blankets for horses. According to Escalante's old-timers, it was always a big event when the Navajos made it to town.

The economic welfare of the Escalante Valley was based mainly on the ranching and timber industries. Early ranchers pioneered many of the routes that are used by hikers and automobiles today. Many canyons and washes are named after these early ranchers: Phipps Wash, Spencer Flat, Moody Canyon, Harris Wash, and Alvey Wash.

After a few years, it became evident that the valley could only support a limited amount of ranching and a few sawmills. The area's population stagnated between 1920 and 1980 as many of the young people were attracted to job opportunities in Salt Lake City. Tourism has recently brought back life to many of the towns of southern Utah.

2

Petroglyphs near Escalante River

Canyons of the Escalante

Overview

L ooking out over the Escalante River Basin from the top of Boulder Mountain, the vast stretches of rock stand out the most. The white color of the Navajo Sandstone and the deep reds of the Wingate can be seen stretching for miles, interrupted only by a few deep and sinuous canyons. The basin is a virtual labyrinth of deep narrow canyons incised into the rock.

HOW THE CANYON OF THE ESCALANTE RIVER FORMED

Many of the rivers of the Colorado Plateau cut unexpectedly across large areas of uplifted rock instead of flowing around them. For instance, the Escalante River flows right through the giant folded uplift of Navajo Sandstone located just to the east of the town of Escalante.

Geologists reason that for this to occur the river must have roughly occupied its present course before the features that it now crosses were uplifted. The river was able to maintain its course by down-cutting into these features at a more rapid rate than the rocks uplifted.

The Escalante River Canyon as we now see it began forming about thirty million years ago when uplift of the Colorado Plateau began. The Navajo Sandstone through which the Escalante River flows is fractured and jointed, and the Escalante took full advantage of these fractures as it eroded into this layer of rock that was slowly being uplifted. For the most part, the meandering course of the river follows the path of pre-existing fractures in the Navajo Sandstone.

As you descend into one of these side canyons, the sweeping views gradually give way until all that is left to see lies within the confines of the narrow canyon walls. Because of this, when you hike in the canyons, you feel almost shut in and estranged from the rest of the world.

The canyons hold many secrets: giant alcoves stained with desert varnish, hiding seeps and hanging gardens, the stately cottonwood trees, and deep-blue pools of water left over from the last rain.

The Escalante River, shrouded by impenetrable sandstone cliffs and a vast maze of side canyons, was the last river in the United States to be discovered. The Escalante River Basin is a large area bounded by Boulder Mountain to the north, the Straight Cliffs to the west, and the Waterpocket Fold to the east. The Escalante River Basin itself is a vast tract of uplifted rock into which the incised canyons of the Escalante have coursed. The Escalante River has been called the "crookedest river in the world." One measurement indicated that thirty-five canyon miles were equal to only fourteen straight-line miles.

Hikes in the region vary considerably from the mostly dry and narrow canyons that drain into the Escalante from the east to the well-watered canyons of the Escalante that drain off Boulder Mountain. Hiking down the Escalante River itself is difficult because of thick brush and numerous river crossings.

The natural beauty of the area was recognized as early as 1936 when the area was included in a proposed 4.5-million-acre national park. Developmental interests killed plans for this park, even though a large amount of support existed, including that of the National Park Service.

HIGHWAY 12—TORREY TO TROPIC:
ROUTE DESCRIPTION

Driving through the slickrock desert between Escalante and Boulder is an experience comparable to seeing Yosemite Valley or the Grand Canyon for the first time. Highway 12 is the main paved

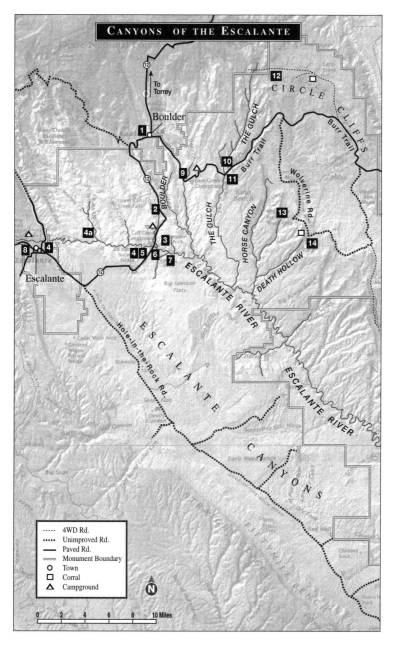

CANYONS OF THE ESCALANTE

To
Torrey

Boulder

CIRCLE CLIFFS

Burr Trail

1

10

9

11

THE GULCH

Burr Trail

Wolverine Rd.

2

BOULDER

4a

3

4 **5** **6**

7

THE GULCH

HORSE CANYON

13

14

8 **4**

Escalante

ESCALANTE RIVER

DEATH HOLLOW

Big Spencer
Flats

Hole-in-the-Rock Rd.

E S C A L A N T E

ESCALANTE RIVER

C A N Y O N S

- - - - - 4WD Rd.
· · · · · Unimproved Rd.
——— Paved Rd.
░░░░ Monument Boundary
○ Town
□ Corral
△ Campground

N

0   2   4   6   8   10 Miles

road through the monument, providing access to Smoky Mountain Road, Burr Trail, Hole-in-the-Rock Road, and Cottonwood Wash Road. It parallels the northern boundary of the monument, passing through Boulder and Escalante.

South of Torrey the road begins a steady climb to the top of Boulder Mountain. It takes at least an hour to drive the thirty-five miles along this steep and winding highway.

The road rises to 9,400 feet as it skirts the top of Boulder Mountain. More a large plateau than a mountain, Boulder Mountain rises to over 11,000 feet and is covered by lakes, aspen, and pine trees. Many of the tributaries of the Escalante begin atop Boulder Mountain, including Steep Creek, Death Hollow, the Gulch, Calf Creek, Boulder Creek, and Sand Creek.

Some of the best views in all of Utah are from the top of Boulder Mountain, and many viewpoints and pullouts exist along the road, which offers views of the Escalante River Basin, the Straight Cliffs, the Circle Cliffs, Capitol Reef National Park, and the Henry Mountains. On a clear day, the La Sal Mountains can be seen to the east more than a hundred miles away.

The road descends from the summit of Boulder Mountain to the town of Boulder, the official park entrance. Boulder, named because of the large basalt boulders found in the area, is a small town with a few gas stations, motels, and a cafe. From here, Highway 12 heads west and Burr Trail takes off to the east (*see* Burr Trail on page 56).

Heading west from Boulder, the highway crosses Boulder Creek before traversing up a series of switchbacks to a large ridge that separates Calf Creek Canyon on the right and Boulder Creek on the left. The ridge gradually narrows until there is barely enough room for the two-lane highway. Cliffs drop off hundreds of feet to either side. Luckily, a few pullouts have been constructed so you can stop and enjoy the expansive views of this sandstone country.

From the top of the ridge, the road makes a steep descent through the Navajo Sandstone to Calf Creek. Lower Calf Creek Campground (3) is located at the bottom of the descent and is a nice place to camp or eat lunch. Continuing from the turnoff to the Lower Calf Creek Campground, it is about two miles to where the highway crosses the

Escalante River. The Escalante River Trailhead (*see* Access on page 43) is located on the right side of the road, just before the highway crosses the river.

The One-Hundred-Hand Pictograph is a short walk from the Escalante River Trailhead (see Escalante River Crossing [5]). This pictograph panel is perhaps the biggest in the monument. Petroglyphs and a small Anasazi ruin can also be seen nearby.

After crossing the Escalante River, Highway 12 begins a steep climb out of the canyon. The road has been blasted out of the sandstone in numerous places, and there are some good viewpoints near the top.

The Navajo Sandstone along Highway 12 is not uniform in color. The lower-elevation material near Calf Creek and the Escalante River is quite red, while the sandstone forming the ridges and bowls above the canyons is white. The different colors are a result of iron-rich groundwaters flowing through certain parts of the Navajo Sandstone.

The numerous canyons and intervening ridges of the Escalante River Basin long served as a barrier to visitors. The present Highway 12 that traverses the region was not completed until 1940, and the section over Boulder Mountain was not completely paved until 1980. Prior to 1940 the only way to get to the town of Boulder was via Hell's Backbone Road, which was completed in 1935. Hell's Backbone Road takes off of Highway 12 about two miles west of Boulder and can be used as an alternative route to Escalante. The road is named after Hell's Backbone, a small bridge along the road that crosses over a narrow ridge separating Death Hollow and Sand Creek. The bridge is barely big enough for two cars, and cliffs drop almost 800 feet on either side to the canyon bottoms below.

After leaving Escalante, Highway 12 enters Main Canyon, which, with its stair-like profile, is very similar to many of the canyons of the Kaiparowits Plateau. Keep an eye out for Indian ruins while traveling up the canyon.

Highway 12 continues upward to a pass between the Kaiparowits Plateau and the Table Mountain Plateau. From the top of the pass, the road makes a steep decline through "The Blues" (30) before reaching the town of Tropic. The Blues refers to an area of plantless badlands primarily composed of Tropic shale. In some places, Tropic shale is a good formation in which to look for marine fossils.

Anasazi State Park (1)

Located in the town of Boulder, this small state park is just outside the boundaries of the Grand Staircase–Escalante National Monument. The Anasazi Coombs Ruins are the highlight of the monument. Museum displays on the Anasazi and Fremont cultures help to provide an understanding of the ruins and rock art found in the monument.

The Coombs site was occupied by the Anasazi between A.D. 1125 and 1170. It was discovered in 1927, and excavations have uncovered ninety-seven rooms and ten pit structures. The village was abandoned about A.D. 1175. Artifacts uncovered at the site are displayed in the museum where exhibits discuss how the Anasazi and Fremont lived and the possible reasons for their abrupt disappearance. The museum is open 9:00 A.M. to 5:00 P.M. daily, longer during the summer, and a $2 entrance fee is charged.

Upper Calf Creek Falls (2)

Overview

This is a steep but short hike to spectacular waterfalls along Calf Creek. Although not quite as long as Lower Calf Creek Falls, the upper falls are still impressive. This hiking trail is easily accessible from Highway 12 and not as heavily used as the trail to Lower Calf Creek Falls.

Access

The turnoff to the Upper Calf Creek trailhead is twenty miles east of Escalante or ten miles west of Boulder, along Highway 12. Look for a small, unmarked dirt road between mileposts 81 and 82 on the west side of the highway. This side road heads west for a quarter mile before ending at the parking area for the Upper Calf Creek Falls trailhead. No signs indicate the location of the trailhead, but a registration box is located at the start of the trail.

Upper Calf Creek

Difficulty

The trail to the falls is a little over a mile but is quite steep with an altitude change of 500 feet. Cairns mark the route, so it is easy to follow.

Map

1:24,000 Calf Creek

Elevation

Top: 6,400 feet
Bottom: 5,900 feet

Water

The water in Calf Creek is drinkable if properly treated.

Camping

The BLM has designated this area as day use only, and no camping is allowed within a half-mile radius of the falls.

Route Description

From the parking area, the trail immediately goes down a steep decline toward the bottom of Calf Creek Canyon. Views of the canyon and the surrounding slickrock country are fantastic before the trail drops into Calf Creek Canyon.

Over the slickrock portions of the trail, large black boulders of basalt have been moved to either side of the trail. These large lava rocks washed down from Boulder Mountain and look conspicuously out of place sitting next to the Navajo Sandstone. The lava rocks date back twenty-five million years to a period when Boulder Mountain was volcanically active.

Continuing downhill, the trail gradually levels out as it passes over more slickrock and sandy sections. Iron-rich pieces of Navajo Sandstone can be seen everywhere; they are black and heavy, and some have weathered into interesting shapes.

The sides of Calf Creek Canyon are covered with pinyon and juniper trees. Oak, cottonwoods, and ponderosa pine grow in the bottom of the canyon where water is available. Manzanita, a shrub with thick, waxy evergreen leaves, grows along the trail. It has small white flowers in the spring.

The trail divides just before reaching the falls. The lower segment leads to the waterfalls, and the upper segment of the trail continues a short distance up Calf Creek to some deep pools that have been carved out of the sandstone. These pools make excellent swimming holes in the hot summer months.

The Upper Calf Creek Falls are eighty-six feet high and pour off a sandstone ledge into a deep pool. Red and green mosses, ferns, and hanging gardens grow on the red-rock walls behind the falls, producing a picturesque blend of colors, a rare find in the desert country. Willows, oak trees, and various grasses create a thick shroud of green vegetation around the pool. Watercress, not seen in many of the monument's canyons, grows around the pool's edge.

Upper Calf Creek Falls

Lower Calf Creek Falls (3)

Overview
Established in 1963, the well-maintained trail to Lower Calf Creek Falls is one of the monument's most popular trails. The trail starts at Calf Creek Campground and heads up Calf Creek to the falls, which cascades over a tall sandstone cliff into a deep-blue pool surrounded by lush vegetation. Several Anasazi ruins and some large pictographs can be seen along this easy hike.

Access
The trailhead is located at Calf Creek Campground, which is sixteen miles east of Escalante along Highway 12, or fourteen miles west of Boulder. The turnoff to Calf Creek Campground is well marked and easily spotted from the highway. A day-use fee of $2 is charged at the parking area.

Difficulty
The hiking is easy along a well-maintained and level trail. The five-and-a-half-mile round-trip to the falls takes about three hours.

Map
1:24,000 Calf Creek

Elevation
5,400 feet to 5,600 feet

Water
It is best to bring your own; water from Calf Creek needs to be treated.

Camping
No camping is allowed along the trail as the area surrounding the lower falls is intended for day use only. Calf Creek Campground, located at the trailhead, is very nice but is quite popular and often full. Alternatives to Calf Creek are Deer Creek Campground (9), located six miles east of Boulder on Burr Trail, and the Escalante Petrified Forest State Park Campground (8).

Lower Calf Creek Falls

Route Description

The hike is a self-guided tour, and a small pamphlet available at the trailhead describes the entire hike in detail, including where to see the ancient Anasazi granaries and pictographs. Binoculars would be useful, as granaries and pictographs are some distance away from the trail. Calf Creek Canyon cuts deep into the surrounding Navajo Sandstone. A small creek meanders through the lush vegetation along the canyon bottom. The trail follows close to the canyon walls on the east side of the canyon but never crosses the creek. Deep alcoves have developed into the sandstone walls, and one of them hides some rather large pictographs.

The canyon gradually narrows, and the last mile of the hike is well shaded by cottonwood, dogwood, and box elder trees. Beavers have built numerous dams along Calf Creek, and brown trout flourish in the ponds that form behind these dams. Beaver are common in the Escalante Canyons that have flowing water, but they are elusive animals that are usually only seen at dawn and dusk.

Approaching the falls, the canyon walls close in, and the humidity rises in the air. The fall cascades 126 feet down a sheer sandstone cliff. The deep pool beneath the falls is surrounded by lush vegetation. Mosses, various ferns, horsetail, sedges, columbine, and monkey flower all grow here, sheltered from the sun by the giant cliffs and protected from dry air by mist from the falls.

The Escalante River Trailhead: Highway 12 Bridge to Escalante (4)

Overview

The fifteen-mile stretch of the Escalante River Canyon between the town of Escalante and Highway 12 contains Anasazi ruins, pictographs, natural bridges, and arches. This stretch of the Escalante River Trail provides access to Death Hollow (14) and Sand Creek tributaries of the Escalante. The Escalante River flows through a deep and beautiful canyon. This is one of the easiest sections of the Escalante River to hike because there is less brush, and stream crossings are relatively simple. Day hikes are possible along the river from either the town of Escalante or from the Escalante River Trailhead. A two- or three-day backpacking trip can be made through the canyon (requires two cars or shuttle).

Access

Escalante River Trailhead

The Escalante River Trailhead is fifteen miles east of the town of Escalante along Highway 12. It is located on the left side of the road just after the highway crosses the Escalante River. If coming from Boulder, proceed two miles past the Calf Creek turnoff and look for the Escalante River Trailhead on the right side of the road just before the highway crosses the river.

Escalante Town Canyon Access

As you head east on Highway 12, drive a quarter mile past the last gas station in the town of Escalante. Then take a left at the junction marked "Escalante River Trailhead." As you leave the highway, drive about another half mile before taking another left; this left turn is marked by a sign indicating the direction to the Escalante River Trailhead. Drive another mile to the end of the road and the trailhead.

Difficulty

The trail along this fifteen-mile stretch of river is easy to follow, but numerous stream crossings and areas of thick brush and vegetation make this a moderately strenuous hike. Most of the difficulties with brush are encountered near the mouth of Death Hollow, which is seven and a half miles upstream from the Escalante River Trailhead. Since there are quite a few stream crossings, be sure to bring appropriate shoes and dry clothes. Long pants are also suggested when hiking through areas of thick brush. The hike is best done in the warmer months as the stream water is quite cold November through February.

Maps

1:24,000 Calf Creek
1:24,000 Escalante

Elevation

Highway 12 (bridge): 5,204 feet
Escalante (town): 5,700 feet

Water

Water from the Escalante River or Death Hollow is fairly good quality but should be treated.

Camping

There are plenty of spots for backpackers to camp within the canyon. Day hikers can camp at one of the nearby campgrounds such as Calf Creek or Escalante State Park.

* A note on day hikes along the Escalante River: The hike down the Escalante River from the town of Escalante goes through the deepest, most scenic stretches of the canyon and passes some large pictographs. Hiking upstream from Highway 12 offers the advantage of seeing the Escalante Natural Bridge, the Escalante Natural Arch, and several large Indian ruins.

Route Description (starting from Escalante River Trailhead)

Heading upstream, the trail almost immediately crosses the river and follows the southern side of the stream for some distance. The canyon near Highway 12 is quite broad, and the rounded sandstone knobs and alcoves that form the canyon walls are set back from the river. Giant cottonwood trees line the river and provide cool shade. The Navajo Sandstone seems to take on a variety of colors ranging from white to orange.

The Escalante Natural Arch and the Escalante Natural Bridge lie in close proximity to one another, about one and a half miles upstream from the trailhead. The Escalante Natural Arch comes into view first along the canyon's skyline, even though the Escalante Natural Bridge is slightly downstream from the arch. The Escalante Natural Bridge is easily seen from the trail and is located in a small side canyon on the left side of the river. The Escalante Natural Bridge, at 130 feet high and 100 feet across, is the largest feature of this type in the monument. The best views of the arch are about a quarter mile upstream from the Natural Bridge.

Large Indian ruins can be seen on the cliff face below Escalante Natural Arch. These ruins are set in an alcove about twenty-five feet up the canyon wall from the river. The two stone structures look well preserved, and burnt juniper logs can be seen forming the roof of one of the structures. The ruins look impossible to reach without some type of ladder.

The river gradually narrows upstream, and Sand Creek enters from the right, about three miles from the trailhead. Sand Creek is a long and winding canyon that drains off Boulder Mountain.

About a mile and a half above the mouth of Sand Creek, the Escalante River, having narrowed and deepened considerably, enters a series of meanders about a mile and a half long. The river's course straightens again a mile before Death Hollow enters the Escalante, but this is difficult to see as the vegetation is quite thick. Hiking is difficult near the mouth of Death Hollow due to numerous stream crossings and thicker vegetation.

Death Hollow is a large side canyon that enters the Escalante from the right. A small trail breaks away from the main trail and goes up Death Hollow (*see* Death Hollow side trip [4a]). Death Hollow would be a difficult canyon not to notice as it has a fairly good-sized stream.

About a mile up the Escalante River from the mouth of Death Hollow the vegetation becomes less dense and the hiking easier. Ponderosa pines grow throughout the canyon. Some of the large pine trees grow right out of the small cracks and fractures that are found in the sandstone walls. Cottonwoods, willows, box elder, tamarisk, and Russian olive trees dominate the bottom of the canyon. Russian olive trees have extremely sharp thorns and are an exotic species like tamarisk.

Above the mouth of Death Hollow, the Escalante River Canyon is fairly straight and open for about three miles. River crossings are easier partly because Death Hollow contributes a lot of water to the Escalante. The Escalante Canyon is at its deepest during the last four miles as it enters another large section of meanders. A large alcove shelters some pictographs about halfway through the four-mile section of meanders. The pictographs are on the opposite side of the river from the main trail but are easily seen. They are painted with a white pigment and are quite large but in poor condition.

Pine Creek enters from the right near the end of the trail. The Escalante above Pine Creek is just a small stream, as Pine Creek and

Death Hollow combined contribute about 70 percent of the water to the Escalante. The trail goes past a water-metering station before leaving the Escalante River and heading south about a half mile to the parking area.

The Boulder Mail Trail, also known as the Death Hollow Trail, takes off to the right just before Pine Creek enters the Escalante. Prior to 1935, this historic trail was the main route between Escalante and Boulder. The Boulder Mail Trail crosses some beautiful country but is difficult hiking. The route is poorly marked, and anybody attempting it should have a good map and map-reading skills. The Boulder Mail Trail shows up on the Escalante Trails map.

The Escalante River Crossing at Highway 12: Pictographs and Ruins (5)

Besides providing access to some of the most popular hiking routes in the monument, the Escalante River trailhead is located in close proximity to displays of pictographs, petroglyphs, and Anasazi ruins. The One-Hundred-Hand Panel is one of the monument's largest and most well-known pictograph panels.

Moki House, Escalante River

To reach the One-Hundred-Hand Panel, park at the Escalante River Trailhead (4). The panel is located on the same side of the river as the trailhead. Walk upstream and along the cliffs, remaining to the right of the small cabin near the parking area. A vague trail can be followed that leads through a wooden gate and up to the pictographs. The pictographs are not along the first set of cliffs near the trailhead but are located farther away from the river on the next set of higher cliffs. This short hike is no more than a quarter mile. Binoculars are advisable as the pictographs are difficult to climb up to. Even without binoculars they are easily visible.

Once the pictograph panel is found, a petroglyph panel is located downstream along the same set of cliffs as the pictographs. An old Anasazi ruin, "Moki House," is also found downstream from the trailhead. To reach the ruin, follow the trail about a hundred yards past the highway bridge and look for it in the canyon walls to the left.

Death Hollow (side trip) (4a)

Overview

This beautiful and isolated side canyon of the Escalante River is located halfway between the town of Escalante and Highway 12 along the Escalante River Trail. Death Hollow Creek flows through a colorful and narrow canyon line. Getting to the mouth of the canyon requires a seven-and-a-half-mile hike one way.

Access (see Escalante River Hike on page 43 for trailhead locations)

Death Hollow is accessed from the Escalante River Trail. The mouth of this side canyon is a seven-and-half-mile hike from either the town of Escalante or from where Highway 12 crosses the Escalante River. The canyon is easily spotted from the Escalante River Trail.

Difficulty

An unmaintained trail heads up the canyon, but it is difficult to follow in areas with thick vegetation. Hiking in Death Hollow requires long stretches of wading through the creek. This may sound

Death Hollow

unpleasant, but the stream is shallow, and on a hot day it is very refreshing.

Maps
1:24,000 Escalante
1:100,000 Escalante

Elevation
5,400 feet to 5,800 feet

Water
The water is very good quality but still needs to be treated.

Camping
A good tent site is found about a mile upstream beneath a large overhang (*see* Route Description below); other sites exist just upstream from this overhang but are not quite as nice.

Route Description
Death Hollow, like the Escalante, forms a deep canyon through the Navajo Sandstone. However, Death Hollow Canyon is narrower than the Escalante. The red canyon walls and cascading creek make for a very enjoyable hike. The creek bed is a combination of boulders, deep-blue pools, moss-covered slickrock, and sandy bottoms, all of which produce a pleasing color contrast.

A dry-fall is located one mile up Death Hollow from the Escalante. A large pool of water has developed beneath the dry-fall, making a good swimming hole, and the rock overhang behind the dry-fall produces an excellent camping area. A few more good camping areas can be found in smaller alcoves just a short distance upstream.

About two miles upstream, the canyon begins to narrow. The river cascades over a series of small falls and plunge pools, which are some of the canyon's most attractive features. Various ferns and mosses grow in the sheltered rock crevices of this deep cool canyon. Numerous beaver tracks are present throughout.

Mamie Creek is a tributary of Death Hollow that takes off to the left about three and a half miles upstream from the Escalante River.

This side canyon is of interest because it provides a route to Mamie Creek Arch. Mamie Creek is a relatively stagnant creek in contrast to the clear-flowing water of Death Hollow. When hiking in this canyon, be sure to watch for poison ivy.

Mamie Creek ends at a large dry-fall a little less than a mile upstream from where it left Death Hollow. A large pool is present below the dry-fall. The sandy rim of the pool makes an excellent camping spot. A very, very steep route on the north side of the pool can be used to get above the dry-fall, thus providing a route to Mamie Creek Arch.

Death Hollow got its name from the numerous livestock that died crossing the canyon. Death Hollow Trail was one of the early routes between Escalante and Boulder. It crosses Death Hollow about seven miles from its junction with the Escalante.

Phipps Wash (6)

Overview

The hike to this beautiful side canyon of the Escalante starts from Highway 12 and heads down the Escalante River before going up Phipps Wash. Maverick and Phipps Arches are located in Phipps Wash and can be seen on this hike. A small creek runs in the lower sections of Phipps Wash, the middle section is quite dry with a flat sandy bottom, and the upper part of the wash traverses long portions of slickrock.

Access

This hike starts at the Escalante River Trailhead, fifteen miles east of Escalante along Highway 12. Immediately after the highway crosses the Escalante River, a sign indicates the turnoff to the Escalante River Trailhead. If coming from Boulder, proceed a mile and a half past the Calf Creek Campground turnoff and look for the Escalante River Trailhead on the right side of the road.

Difficulty

The route follows a well-maintained trail from the Escalante River Trailhead to Phipps Wash, a distance of just over a mile. The trail crosses the Escalante River once on the way to Phipps Wash.

Phipps Wash

This crossing is simple but requires knee-deep wading. Except for a few places where the vegetation is a little thick, hiking is easy in Phipps Wash along a well-used footpath. The entire length of Phipps Wash is roughly four miles.

Map
1:24,000 Calf Creek

Elevation
5,200 feet to 5,500 feet

Water
The water in the Escalante River carries some sediment but is drinkable. The water in Phipps Wash is clear and drinkable but may be a little stagnant.

Camping
No camping is allowed between the Escalante River and the mouth of Phipps Wash because the trail cuts through private property. Backpackers can set up camp at the junction of Phipps Wash and the Escalante River, and other possible camping sites exist up Phipps Wash. Car campers can use Calf Creek Campground, which is a mile east of the Escalante River Trailhead on Highway 12.

Route Description
Follow the trail downstream along the left side of the Escalante River. The trail cuts across private property for the first mile, but this is not a problem as the property owners have granted an easement for the trail. The Escalante River is crossed one time before reaching Phipps Wash. This crossing is indicated by a BLM sign.

The side canyon of Phipps Wash enters the Escalante River Canyon about a mile and a half downstream from the trailhead. Phipps Wash is the first large wash to enter the Escalante from the right. A half mile before reaching Phipps Wash, a sign marks the entrance to the Escalante Outstanding Natural Area.

A footpath can be followed up the lower part of Phipps Wash. The small creek in Phipps Wash is lined with cottonwood trees, and deep clear pools fill depressions in the streambed. Frogs live in some of these pools and can be heard at night if you camp in the area. When the pools dry up, these desert frogs bury themselves in the mud and wait for the next rain.

Maverick Bridge is a short distance up the first side canyon, on the right side of Phipps Wash. This side canyon is about one-third of a mile up Phipps Wash from the Escalante River. Phipps Arch, another impressive arch, lies high on a ridge above Phipps Wash. This arch is difficult to find without using the 1:24,000 map, and finding the route is left to the reader.

Phipps Wash undergoes a dramatic change about a mile above the Escalante River as the little creek disappears and its place is taken by a large sandy wash. The small trail that goes up Phipps Wash disappears here, but the route up the canyon remains easy to follow. Windblown sand fills the wash bottom and created the sand dunes that line the base of the canyon cliffs.

Phipps Wash divides two and a half miles from the Escalante River. Up the wash to the right, you will encounter a large dry-fall after a half mile. The dry-fall is circumnavigated by following a route out of the wash, which is found roughly 150 feet before the dry-fall on the right side of the canyon. The large well-sheltered pool at the bottom of this dry-fall stays covered with ice until April or May.

Above the dry-fall, the steep canyon walls of Phipps Wash give way to expansive views of the large slickrock basin that Phipps Wash drains. Within this large circular basin, Phipps Wash divides so many times that you are best off choosing whatever route looks most interesting. Ponderosa pines grow in the joints of the Navajo Sandstone, which takes on a rounded dome-like appearance. The walking surface in the upper section of Phipps Wash is divided about fifty-fifty between slickrock and sand.

Near the head of Phipps Wash, numerous perfectly round iron concretions can be found weathering within the Navajo Sandstone. These iron concretions are black and heavy, varying in size from as small as a marble to as large as a tennis ball. Concretions are common in sandstone and form because minerals are precipitated from the groundwater that gradually moves through the rock.

Escalante Petrified Forest State Park (8)

This state park, famous for its well-preserved and colorful specimens of petrified wood, is located on the north side of Highway 12 one mile west of the town of Escalante. A nice campground with showers, picnic tables, fire pits, and reasonable prices is located here. The campground is right next to Wide Hollow Reservoir, and state park officials rent out canoes for use on the lake, which often has good fishing. A number of well-preserved and colorful specimens of petrified wood can be seen right within the campground area.

Hiking trails can be used in the monument to find petrified wood. The main trail is an easy one-mile loop with an optional loop that is three-quarters of a mile long and somewhat steep.

The petrified wood was deposited in ancient floodplains about 140 million years ago. The wood was quickly buried on the floodplains of ancient rivers, which contributed to its preservation. The area was later covered by volcanic ash that was rich in minerals. Groundwater became saturated in these minerals as it flowed through the volcanic deposits. The mineral-rich groundwater then flowed through the buried wood, depositing various minerals and elements that gave the wood its colors. When this wood was deposited, Utah was very near the equator and the area was much more tropical and humid.

Boynton Arch (7)

Overview

Boynton Arch is an easy hike down the Escalante River to Deer Canyon, a side canyon of the Escalante containing a large arch. It is an easy day hike, and a variety of pictographs and petroglyphs can be seen along the trail.

Access

Same as Phipps Wash (6).

Difficulty

Walking down the Escalante and up Deer Canyon is fairly easy. The Escalante River is crossed twice on the way to Deer Canyon. The knee-deep waters of the Escalante are usually easy to cross.

Map
1:24,000 Calf Creek

Elevation
5,200 feet to 5,400 feet

Water
There is lots of sediment in the Escalante; large pools in Deer Canyon contain water but are usually stagnant.

Camping
Backpackers can camp near the mouth of Phipps Canyon or up Deer Canyon.

Route Description
Follow the Escalante River downstream from the trailhead. The trail goes through private property for the first mile. A sign about halfway to Deer Canyon indicates the entrance to the Escalante Outstanding Natural Area. The Escalante River is crossed twice before reaching Phipps Wash (6) and once after; the first crossing is indicated by a BLM sign.

It is about two miles to the mouth of Deer Canyon, which is known locally but not labeled on the map. Deer Canyon is the first large canyon to enter the Escalante from the left, and its wide mouth is easily seen from the trail.

A large petroglyph panel is located on a large rock outcrop on the right-hand side of the mouth of Deer Canyon. Some brilliantly red pictographs are located up Deer Canyon about halfway to the arch, on the right side of the canyon near the streambed. There are more pictographs near the head of Deer Canyon, past Boynton Arch, and their location can be found on the Calf Creek map.

Deer Creek Canyon is lined by tall red-sandstone walls. Deep-blue pools have gouged out the sandstone wash. It is a mile walk up Deer Canyon from the Escalante River to Boynton Arch.

Phipps Wash and Boynton Arch are named after early cattle ranchers. Phipps and Boynton had a shoot-out in the 1890s over a ranching dispute near the present location of where Highway 12 crosses the Escalante River. Phipps was killed and is buried somewhere near the One-Hundred-Hand Panel.

BURR TRAIL: ROUTE DESCRIPTION

Burr Trail is one of the most scenic and easily accessible drives in the monument. It heads east from Highway 12 at Boulder. No services are found along this sixty-six-mile stretch of road that connects Highway 12 to Highway 276. Burr Trail is paved but turns to dirt once it leaves the monument's boundaries.

Burr Trail was originally developed in the early 1880s by John Burr, who used the trail to move cattle from summer to winter ranges. Uranium miners improved the road in the 1950s as they scoured the Circle Cliffs for uranium deposits. The road was paved during the 1980s, but a seventeen-mile section within Capitol Reef remains unpaved. Environmentalists have fought against any improvements to the Burr Trail, and the remaining unpaved section of the road can be credited to their efforts.

Heading east from Boulder, Burr Trail enters a land of sandstone domes and canyons. Near Boulder, the elevation is high enough for ponderosa pines to grow within the cracks and joints of the Navajo Sandstone and along the wash bottoms.

Burr Trail crosses Deer Creek (9) six and a half miles east of Boulder where the BLM maintains a campground with tables, barbecue pits, and an outhouse. Short hikes can be made up or down this tributary of the Escalante.

The road makes a steep decline ten and a half miles east of Boulder into the deep canyon called the Gulch (10 & 11). As the road enters the Gulch, the creamy-white Navajo Sandstone gives way to the dark-red sandstones of the Kayenta and Wingate Formations. The Gulch is one of Escalante's more-scenic side canyons, with long stretches of tall red cliffs.

Continuing east, Burr Trail exits the Gulch and enters Long Canyon. Like the Gulch, Long Canyon cuts through dark-red cliffs of Wingate Sandstone. The tall cliffs, desert varnish, large alcoves, and a relatively narrow canyon bottom make this stretch of Burr Trail one of the best drives in the monument. The road follows Long Canyon for seven miles before the canyon ends near the rim of the Circle Cliffs.

From the top of the Circle Cliffs, the Henry Mountains and the Waterpocket Fold can be seen in the far distance, but views of the Circle Cliffs overshadow all else. They stretch for miles to the north and south. The road then follows a steep grade down from the rim of the cliffs to the flats below.

Nineteen miles east of Boulder, Wolverine Road heads south from Burr Trail and is well marked. This road continues along the base of the Circle Cliffs and eventually reconnects with a southern spur of Burr Trail. Wolverine Road can be used to access a number of the side canyons of the Escalante River as well as the Wolverine Petrified Wood Area *(see* description of Wolverine Road on page 66).

East of the junction with Wolverine Road, Burr Trail extends to the east through a maze of small washes and buttes covered by a forest of pinyon pine and juniper trees. About twenty-two miles east of Boulder, another side road heads off toward the Lamp Stand and the upper part of the Gulch. (This side road is described in the section on Lamanite Arch [12] on page 64).

Another major junction is found thirty miles east of Boulder. A well-used road heads to the right toward Moody Creek and Silver Falls Creek. This fairly good dirt road reconnects with Wolverine Road, making a loop *(see* map on page 33). Burr Trail continues to the east and enters Capitol Reef National Park. The entrance to Capitol Reef is quite dramatic as Burr Trail descends through Waterpocket Fold in a series of switchbacks.

Deer Creek Campground (9)

This is a nice campground with tables, fire pits, and restrooms. The campground has a limited number of sites, but it is usually not as crowded as the campground at Lower Calf Creek. Although this is a no-fee campground, the BLM asks for a small donation for staying here.

The campground is a nice place to stay, located next to a running creek and set among the white domes of Navajo Sandstone. Hikers may hike up or down Deer Creek, and those who look can find one of the petroglyph panels in the canyon. Deer Creek Canyon should not be confused with Deer Creek described in the Boynton Arch hike, as they are separate canyons.

Upper Gulch (10)

Overview

The Gulch is one of the larger tributaries of the Escalante to cross Burr Trail. With easy access from Boulder, the Gulch is well known for its beautiful canyon walls and running water. Stream crossings are easy, and a fairly well-used trail makes for easy walking. A number of side canyons allow for exploration, and a backpacking trip can be made to Lamanite Arch.

Access

The Gulch is located ten and a half miles east of Boulder along Burr Trail, which makes a steep decline into the canyon of the Gulch. A BLM sign indicates the parking area for the trailhead.

Difficulty

The route is easy walking along sandy trails. The small stream is easily crossed without getting your feet wet. Lamanite Arch is about ten miles up the Gulch and makes a good destination for a backpacking trip.

Maps

1:100,000 Escalante
1:24,000 King Bench, Steep Creek Bench

Elevation

Top: 6,400 feet
Bottom: 5,560 feet

Water

Water in the Gulch carries a lot of sediment. Water Canyon and Indian Hollow, side canyons of the Gulch, have small streams with clear-running water.

Camping

The established campground at Deer Creek (9) is a good location. Sites for backpackers also exist along the route.

The Gulch

Route Description

It is possible to hike either up or down the Gulch. This route description describes the section of the Gulch upstream from Burr Trail. Starting from the parking area, follow the paved road to where it crosses the creek and then continue up the canyon along an unmaintained trail on the right side of the stream.

Steep Creek enters from the left, just short of a mile upstream from the road. This side canyon has a very small stream. Steep Creek can be followed for many miles and makes a good side trip. It has a steeper gradient than the Gulch, and the canyon walls never get as high as those of the Gulch.

The Gulch gradually narrows upstream after the intersection with Steep Creek as it passes through the tall red cliffs of Wingate Sandstone. A small waterfall and plunge pools mark an interesting transition as the canyon begins to cut into the softer Chinle Formation. The waterfall is most easily negotiated on the left side of the canyon.

The canyon begins to widen as it cuts into the less-resistant Chinle Formation. The cliffs of the more-resistant Wingate Sandstone, now perched atop the slope-forming Chinle Formation, are still the most striking features of the canyon. Ponderosa pine trees are scattered sparsely about the base of the cliffs, and oak and cottonwood trees grow in the shelter provided by giant alcoves that have formed into the cliffs.

Above the waterfalls the trail is located on the river terraces ten to fifteen feet above the streambed on the left side of the canyon. Walking is easy on the flat stream terraces, and the trail is easily followed.

Water Canyon enters from the left, four miles upstream from the road. This steep canyon heads west through the deep cliffs of Wingate Sandstone. It is quite a difficult canyon to hike, but the tall canyon walls and the numerous springs and seeps that give rise to the verdant plant life more than make up for the difficulties. Up the Gulch past Water Canyon, the trail is rarely used and is quite faint.

Indian Hollow Canyon enters the Gulch from the left, about eight miles upstream from the trailhead. Lamanite Arch is about a mile and a half up this small canyon. Indian Hollow Canyon is filled with brush and the walking is difficult. Lamanite Arch makes a very long day hike from Burr Trail but would be a good overnight backpacking trip. Alternatively, Lamanite Arch can be more easily reached by using Lamp Stand Road (*see* Lamanite Arch [12]).

Erosional processes are often thought of being slow and gradual, but in the Southwest more rapid erosional events occur, resulting from heavy rainfall and subsequent flash flooding. These rapid events can dramatically alter the landscape by cutting new stream channels or by depositing vast amounts of sediment.

The distribution of cottonwood trees in the Gulch is evidence of a recent erosional event in which the stream channel was lowered five to ten feet. Two generations of trees exists, and the older trees all grow on terraces seven to fifteen feet above the streambed, while the younger trees all grow in the current streambed. The stream must have rapidly down-cut its channel, leaving the established trees stranded on a terrace above the new stream channel. These trees already had a deep root system that allowed them to continue to survive, but younger trees were unable to colonize the stream terrace because of the root depth required to reach water.

Lower Gulch (11)

Overview
This is an easily reached tributary of the Escalante. A small stream provides water for numerous cottonwood trees and a virtual garden of other water-loving plants. The canyon walls of the Lower Gulch are beautifully textured and colored.

Access
It is located ten and a half miles east of Boulder along the Burr Trail, which makes a steep decline into the Gulch. A marked parking area for the trailhead is located on the right side of the road.

Difficulty
Hiking is easy in the Lower Gulch along a well-used but unmaintained trail. The trail is mostly flat and sandy, and stream crossings are simple. It is about twelve miles from the road to the Escalante River, but the last four miles go through some sections of narrows that are difficult to get around. The location of the difficulties is marked as a waterfall on the 1:24,000 map.

Map
1:24,000 King Bench

Elevation
Top: 5,560 feet
Bottom: 5,000 feet

Water
The water in the stream carries some sediment but can be drinkable. It is best to carry your own water.

Camping
Established campsites exist at Deer Creek Campground, located about two miles west from the trailhead along Burr Trail. Backpackers will be able to find good campsites within the Gulch.

Lower Gulch

Route Description

Downstream from the trailhead, the red canyon walls of the Kayenta Formation quickly give way to the more rounded and subdued forms of the Navajo Sandstone. The canyon is fairly wide, but the colorful and beautifully textured sandstone walls make up for it. The canyon has long been appreciated for its beauty and was declared an "outstanding scenic area" by the BLM long before its inclusion within the monument.

The water forming the small stream supports a variety of plants and trees. Cottonwood trees grow quite thick in places, and willows, grasses, and horsetail grow beside the streambed.

Roughly three miles downstream from the trailhead, you will pass an old cabin and corral. Some shallow caves are present on the left side of the canyon across the river from these landmarks. Another mile past the cabin, the canyon turns and heads east and continues on an eastward track for another mile before turning back to the south. At this turn, a large side canyon enters the Gulch.

A good campsite is found just a short distance downstream from where the large side canyon enters the Gulch. The campsite is located under a large cottonwood tree, just upstream from an easily visible and distinctive rock pedestal.

Downstream from the rock pedestal, the trail crosses an old fence line, and a quarter mile below the fence is a cattleman's cabin, which is still in use. Some petroglyphs can be seen on the left side of the Gulch a half mile downstream from the cabin.

Downstream from the petroglyphs, the canyon rapidly narrows, and a dry-fall located a mile and a half from the petroglyphs is a serious obstacle. This dry-fall is best avoided by exiting the canyon to the right and utilizing a route on Brigham Tea Bench. The dry-fall shows up on the 1:24,000 map and it is suggested that this map be used for route-finding if you are attempting to travel downstream past the dry-falls.

Lamanite Arch (12)

Overview

A beautiful arch, giant alcoves, and petrified wood are some of the highlights of this moderately difficult hike. Lamanite Arch is located in Indian Hollow, a side canyon of the Upper Gulch. This arch can also be reached by hiking directly up the Gulch from Burr Trail *(see* Upper Gulch [10] on page 58). The trailhead is about an hour's drive from Boulder, and getting there requires driving north of Burr Trail on a series of dirt roads into a remote area of the monument.

Access

To get to the trailhead, follow Burr Trail twenty-two and a half miles east from Boulder and take a left at the sign indicating, "Lamp Stand five miles." The first junction along this dirt road is a mile and a half north of Burr Trail. From this junction, continue on toward the Lamp Stand. An old corral is present at the second junction, five miles past the first junction. Take a right at the old corral and continue another three miles over a small pass through the Circle Cliffs. The road comes down from this small pass and enters the broad canyon of the Gulch. Take a left on a jeep trail that heads down the canyon. The jeep trail is located just a short distance before the main road crosses the small stream of the Gulch. Walk or drive down this jeep trail about a mile to the Wilderness Study Area (WSA) boundary. Except for the jeep trail, the dirt roads are in good shape and can be traveled by a passenger car.

Difficulty

The easiest route runs along or within the small stream that flows down the Gulch. No established route exists, but the hiking is not difficult. Indian Hollow, the side canyon leading to the arch, is full of brush, and the hiking here is more challenging. Your shoes will get wet from walking in the small creek, and long pants are advisable for walking through the brush. The hike to the arch and back is roughly seven and a half miles.

Maps

1:100,000 Escalante
1:24,000 Steep Creek Bench

Lamanite Arch

Elevation
Top: 6,400 feet
Bottom: 6,200 feet

Water
Indian Hollow Canyon has a spring-fed stream that contains clear cold water. Treat or boil this water before drinking it. The water in the Gulch has some sediment in it.

Camping
Good sites for car camping can be found on the jeep trail, and good sites for backpackers exist along the hike, except in Indian Hollow Canyon where thick brush fills the canyon.

Route Description
Starting from the junction of the jeep trail and the main road, follow the jeep trail down the Gulch about a mile to the WSA boundary.

A faint road continues a quarter mile past the marked boundary. Continue down the Gulch about two miles until the first side canyon, Indian Hollow, appears on the right. Before arriving at this side canyon, you will pass two large alcoves on the right side of the canyon. These intriguing alcoves hide springs and seeps as well as a number of cottonwood trees.

Impossible Peak is a significant landmark in the area, and good views can be seen up the canyon. The white top of this imposing peak is made of Navajo Sandstone.

The Gulch is lined by steep red cliffs of Wingate Sandstone. Beneath the sandstone, the colorful Chinle Formation makes up the creek bed and stream terraces. Exposed petrified logs of up to thirty feet can be seen within the formation. The best places to look for petrified wood are up the broad side canyons on the east side of the Gulch.

Lamanite Arch is located a mile and a half up Indian Hollow Canyon. Hiking in this side canyon is much slower than in the main canyon, due to thicker vegetation. Springs at the head of Indian Hollow form a crystal-clear stream that runs the entire length of the canyon. Willows, tamarisk, cottonwoods, and horsetails grow in abundance along the streambed. Ponderosa pine and Douglas fir trees are present in the upper part of the canyon.

A large alcove with beautifully colored cliffs is located on the left about a half mile before the arch. Lamanite Arch bridges a small side canyon and is visible from the bottom of the wash.

BURR TRAIL SIDE TRIP—WOLVERINE ROAD: ROUTE DESCRIPTION

Wolverine Road traverses the base of the Circle Cliffs, providing access to a number of side canyons of the Escalante as well as the Wolverine Petrified Wood Area. To reach Wolverine Road, drive nineteen and a half miles east from Boulder along Burr Trail before taking a right at a marked intersection. Most vehicles can handle this road, but those with low clearance will need to travel slowly.

Uranium deposits were discovered in the Chinle Formation in the 1950s, and the area was heavily prospected for about fifteen years.

The Chinle is the multicolored, slope-forming formation that is seen at the base of the Circle Cliffs. Prospectors built this road and others to Silver Falls Creek and Impossible Peak to access uranium deposits. Many of the other less-traveled routes in the area were also first engineered by uranium miners. Located at the head of Silver Falls Creek, Hinesville was the largest of several uranium mining camps during the period. The Hinesville camp even had electric lights and an airstrip.

Six miles south of Burr Trail, Horse Canyon appears on the right side of the road. It is the first major canyon to cut through the Circle Cliffs, and a jeep trail takes off from the main road and heads eight miles down Horse Canyon before ending. Some good spots for car camping exist along the way. The canyon holds water during wet spells and near its mouth. The last few miles of Horse Canyon between Death Hollow (two miles past the end of the jeep trail) and the Escalante River are good hiking.

Wolverine Road continues south along the flanks of the Circle Cliffs, passing a number of tributaries of the Escalante that cut through the Circle Cliffs, including Wolverine Creek (13), Death Hollow (14), and the North Fork of Silver Falls Creek. The canyons that drain through the Circle Cliffs provide good hiking; all of them narrow within a few miles of the main road.

The area around the base of Wolverine Creek has long been known for petrified-wood deposits. Most of the petrified wood here is purple and black and not as colorful as that in the Petrified Wood State Park near Escalante, but you can find pieces up to thirty feet in length. Petrified wood is found in the multicolored slope forming Chinle Formation. The wood was deposited on floodplains during the Triassic period, about 190 million years ago. It is about fifty million years older than the petrified wood at Escalante Petrified Forest State Park.

After passing the North Fork of Silver Falls Creek, the road turns east and heads away from the Circle Cliffs. About six miles past Death Hollow is a major three-way junction. To get back to Burr Trail, take a left. Otherwise, take a right toward Moody Creek and Silver Falls Creek. The road is good for the first few miles to Silver Falls Creek, but a high-clearance four-wheel-drive is needed to reach Moody Creek. Deer Point, the highest point along the Waterpocket Fold, is reached by driving toward it via Moody Creek; it makes a good destination for adventurous travelers. Topographic maps show four-wheel-drive roads leading to the base of Deer Point.

Wolverine Creek (13)

Overview

This is an easy hike in a beautiful canyon that cuts through the Circle Cliffs. Giant alcoves and overhangs, small pools, and huge cliffs stained by desert varnish are but some of the high points of the hike. Wolverine Creek is about an hour's drive from Boulder via dirt and paved roads. This canyon and the surrounding ones are excellent places to see large pieces of petrified wood.

Access

Follow Wolverine Road ten and a half miles south from Burr Trail to Wolverine Creek. A sign indicates the parking area for the Wolverine Creek trailhead.

Difficulty

This is an easy hike on sandy trails and along the bottom of the wash. It is a five-mile hike to the junction of Wolverine Creek and Horse Canyon. Wolverine Creek narrows after two miles, and the last three miles are the most interesting.

Maps

1:24,000 Pioneer Mesa
1:24,000 King Bench

Elevation

Top: 5,400 feet
Bottom: 5,040 feet

Water

It is best to bring your own water as it is present only intermittently in Wolverine Creek.

Wolverine Petrified Wood Area

Camping

If you are backpacking, there is good camping at the junction of Wolverine Creek and Horse Canyon. Some of the alcoves in the creek also make good camping spots.

Route Description

The hike down Wolverine Creek starts at the base of the Circle Cliffs. Near the trailhead, the canyon is wide and open with the high walls of the Circle Cliffs on either side. Wolverine Creek narrows considerably after two miles.

The broad canyon results from the more-easily erodible Chinle lying beneath the more-resistant Wingate Sandstone. The Chinle Formation is quickly eroded, and as it erodes it undermines the cliffs of Wingate Sandstone, resulting in their collapse. The large alcoves that form in the Wingate are also a result of this same process *(see* How Do Cliffs Form? on page 23).

Wolverine Creek

The South Fork of Wolverine Creek enters from the left after about two miles. Downstream, Wolverine Creek has running water in places, and cottonwoods dot the canyon floor. The amount of petrified wood in this canyon is amazing and most is quite well preserved. I found logs up to thirty-five feet long in one of the side canyons.

The last few miles of Wolverine Creek are quite narrow, only five feet wide in places. The narrows are not as long or as deep as those in Death Hollow (14), the next canyon cutting through the Circle Cliffs to the south. However, the large alcoves and steep canyon walls of Wolverine Creek provide a spectacular experience. The lips of the large alcoves are stained with water and must turn into impressive waterfalls when storms are in the area. A long day hike or a two-day trip can be made by walking down Wolverine Creek to Horse Canyon and then heading back to Wolverine Road via Horse Canyon and Death Hollow.

Death Hollow (14)

Overview
This canyon has the best sections of narrows on the east side of the Escalante River. Indian petroglyphs, intricately textured sandstone walls, and petrified wood are a few of its interesting features. Death Hollow is easily accessible from Wolverine Road.

Access
Follow Wolverine Road thirteen and a half miles south from Burr Trail to Death Hollow. An old corral is present at Death Hollow's parking area.

Difficulty
The first four miles are fairly easy walking. The last three and a half miles of the canyon are more difficult because the narrow sections of the canyon contain choke stones and dry-falls that require scrambling to get past. Hiking the entire canyon, seven and a half miles one way, is a long day hike.

Maps
1:24,000 Red Breaks
1:24,000 Silver Falls Bench
1:24,000 Pioneer Mesa

Elevation
Top: 5,560 feet
Bottom: 4,960 feet

Water
Water runs intermittently in Death Hollow and needs treatment. It is best to carry in all water.

Camping
Backpackers can find good camping near the junction with Horse Canyon.

Route Description
Death Hollow, like Wolverine Creek, starts as a broad canyon, cutting through the Circle Cliffs on its way to the Escalante River. Juniper, sage, and rabbitbrush grow on the broad stream terraces above the wash, along with Russian thistle and cheat grass, exotic species that attest to overgrazing. Large boulders of Wingate Sandstone have broken from the cliffs, littering the slopes and floor of the canyon below.

The South Fork of Death Hollow enters from the left after a mile and a half of easy walking. Keep an eye out for the petroglyphs that are located on a boulder that has fallen down from the cliffs. This large boulder is very close to the trail and just a short way down the wash from where the South Fork of Death Hollow enters. The rock art shows depictions of snakes, sheep, and other animals, as well as a figure on a pedestal that is about a foot high.

A mile down from the petroglyphs, the canyon begins to narrow, and small pools of water appear in the wash as the variety of plant life increases. In sharp contrast to the drought-tolerant plants near the parking area, the lower canyon contains gambel oak, cotton-wood, pinyon pine, and tamarisk. Some small alcoves contain seeps that provide water for ferns and mosses. The seeps are located along the contact between Wingate Sandstone and the Chinle Formation.

Downstream, the red cliffs of Wingate Sandstone slowly narrow in on the wash, and a number of long sections of narrows are present over the next three miles. Some of the narrows are quite deep and very impressive. No serious obstacles exist, but a few choke stones and dry-falls require some scrambling. These narrows would be much more difficult to hike through if there were a lot of water in the canyon.

The narrows end about a mile before the junction with Horse Canyon, and Death Hollow begins to gradually widen as a result of the creek bed cutting into the Kayenta Formation. Approaching Horse Canyon, red rounded domes of Navajo Sandstone can be seen topping the ridges of the canyon.

A very good campsite exists on the right side of Horse Canyon, about a quarter of a mile from its junction with Death Hollow. Just upstream from this campsite there is an old line cabin and the end of the jeep trail that goes through most of Horse Canyon. Water is found in the lower reaches of the canyon but is less likely to be found farther upstream.

3

Straight Cliffs

The Kaiparowits Plateau

Overview

The Kaiparowits Plateau, the central core of the Grand Staircase–Escalante National Monument, occupies an area larger than that of all of Utah's other national parks combined. This large plateau tilts generally north and merges with the taller Aquarius Plateau. Hence the meaning of the Paiute word *Kaiparowits*, "Big mountain's little brother."

The Kaiparowits Plateau is one of the most isolated wilderness areas in the United States—a land of crumbling rock pillars, mesas, barren cliffs, badlands, and incised canyons. The plateau is penetrated only by dirt roads, most of them four-wheel-drive, and the last permanent inhabitants of the area were the Anasazi of a thousand years ago. Although the area is not an official wilderness area, it is wilderness in the truest sense of the word.

Physical barriers and geographic isolation have long kept people out of the region despite enormous deposits of high-grade coal. Smoky Mountain Road connecting Escalante to Big Water is the only good dirt road on the plateau, and it can take up to five hours to drive the seventy-eight miles between Escalante at the north end of the road and Big Water at the south end. The Straight Cliffs, up to 1,000 feet high, form the eastern boundary of the plateau, and in their fifty-mile length are breached by only one four-wheel-drive road connecting Smoky Mountain Road to Hole-in-the-Rock Road.

The sheer size and isolation of the plateau makes it an excellent wildlife habitat. Black bears and mountain lions live at the higher elevations, and deer and antelope are seen throughout the area. The distribution of plants and wildlife is largely determined by the amount of available water in this arid region.

The plateau was a point of cultural interfacing between the Fremont and Anasazi. Ruins are scattered about the plateau, and sites include masonry villages and rock art. Many of the ruins atop the plateau are simply rock rings and lithic fragments that are found on the flats of the plateau. Some sites probably remain undiscovered, and the adventurous traveler has a good chance of stumbling onto an ancient ruin or rock-art site along one of the many canyon bottoms adjacent to the hundreds of miles of four-wheel-drive routes.

Coal Mines on the Kaiparowits?

The plateau has long been a battleground between developers and conservationists. According to the Utah Geological Survey, there are 11.3 billion tons of recoverable coal buried beneath the plateau. The monetary value of this coal is placed between $221 and $312 billion.

Energy companies first expressed interest in mining this coal in the early 1960s, and construction of a large power plant and coal mine was proposed in the early 1970s. This coal mine would have been enormous, staffing up to 2,000 miners. A new city with an estimated 15,000 people would have been built near the present location of the town of Big Water.

The environmental impact statement for this project was issued in 1976, and it outlined many potential environmental problems with the plans for the proposed power plant and coal mine. Energy interests abandoned the project, claiming that the threat of environmental lawsuits and government delays had resulted in the project becoming too costly.

Perhaps the real reason for the project not going forward was the geographic isolation and physical barriers that made the project so difficult. Energy companies often pointed out that this was an all-or-nothing deal, and a profit could only be made on Kaiparowits coal if the project was of massive scale. Environmentalists may have

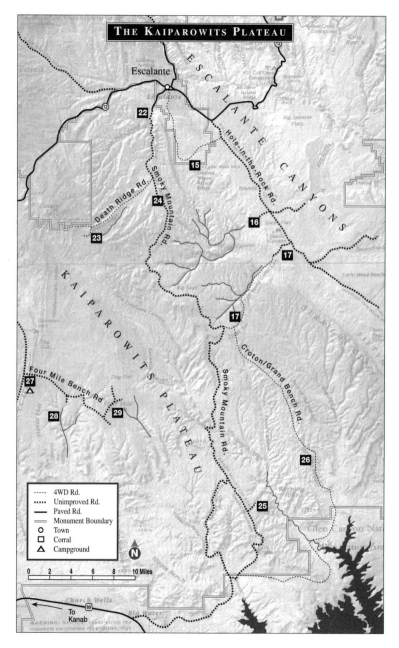

The Kaiparowits Plateau

thwarted and slowed the efforts of the coal miners, but the geographic isolation of the area and the physical barrier of the plateau may have been the real reason for the project's failure.

During the 1980s, coal companies showed a renewed interest in Kaiparowits coal, but this time the plan was to ship the coal to a distant power plant instead of building a plant on the plateau. Required environmental studies were already under way when the area was included in the Grand Staircase–Escalante National Monument. Coal companies withdrew their mining claims soon after the area was declared part of the national monument.

Currently, 10 percent of the monument is under lease for oil and gas exploration. Recently, a controversial oil well was drilled on the Kaiparowits Plateau near the area referred to as "East of the Navajos," but this drilling project was unsuccessful, and it appears unlikely that more projects will be attempted.

SMOKY MOUNTAIN ROAD: ROUTE DESCRIPTION

This graded dirt road connects Escalante along Highway 12 and Big Water along Highway 89. Traveling the seventy-eight miles of road can take up to five hours, and the drive is best made in a high-clearance vehicle, not because the road is impassable to normal passenger cars but because the driving time would be greatly increased in a passenger vehicle. Do not attempt to drive this road during periods of bad weather or when the road is muddy or icy.

Heading south from Escalante, Smoky Mountain Road travels up Alvey Wash, a large canyon that varies in depth from 600 to 800 feet. The canyon walls are composed of the Straight Cliffs Formation, which is made up of multiple layers of sandstone and shale. The sandstone is more resistant to erosion and forms small cliffs and ledges while the shale forms the slopes between the ledges, thus giving the canyon a staircase-type look.

Coal Canyon (22) enters Alvey Wash on the right, four miles south of Escalante. This is a good canyon to walk to get a general feel for the Kaiparowits Plateau. The canyon walls of both Alvey Wash and Coal Canyon are lined with juniper, pinyon pine, and oak trees, and

Smoky Mountain Road

Alvey Wash

Horse Canyon

even a few ponderosa pine trees grow on the north-facing slopes. The washes of Alvey and Coal Canyons have a small amount of water, allowing a few cottonwoods to grow along the canyon bottoms.

Beautiful red-painted pictographs can be found in Alvey Wash. South of Escalante, look for them on the right side of the road just before the mouth of Coal Canyon. Another panel that is worth finding is on the left side of the canyon between Calf and Coal Canyon. The pictographs depict red-painted human handprints and human-like figures. Up Calf Canyon, a large arch is visible from the road. Horse Canyon, another tributary of Alvey Wash, has several Indian ruins and is an interesting canyon to explore.

Eight miles south of Escalante, Death Ridge Road branches off Smoky Mountain Road to the left. This maintained road is used to access Trap Canyon (23) and Death Ridge, which is one of the highest points on the plateau; there are good views in all directions from the top.

Continuing past the junction with Death Ridge Road, Smoky Mountain Road follows Alvey Wash to the top of the Kaiparowits Plateau. From here, large buttes and eroding mesas and ridges can be seen in the distance. The plateau top is home to expansive pinyon-juniper forests, visible for miles. Many of the deep canyons that cut into the plateau can be seen from the road. The most interesting of these are Sarah Ann Canyon, Carcass Canyon, and the Left Hand of Collet Canyon (17), which deepen to the east and cut down through the plateau toward the base of the Straight Cliffs.

A mile after passing the left-hand fork of Collet Canyon, you will encounter a major junction. It cannot be missed because a cattleman's cabin and corral sit right at the intersection. The road splits, with Smoky Mountain Road continuing to the right and the road to Collet Top Junction branching to the left.

It is another three miles to Collet Top Junction. From there it is possible to go south on Croton Road (*see* description on page 102), which provides an alternate route to Big Water, or north down the left-hand fork of Collet Canyon (17), which connects with Hole-in-the-Rock Road.

Driving south on Smoky Mountain Road, it is easy to become almost mesmerized by the sheer size and vastness of the Kaiparowits Plateau. Last Chance Creek, fifteen miles south of the cattleman's cabin, is named because it was the last place that cattlemen crossing the plateau could get any water. Giant cottonwoods line the creek bed, and their green leaves seem out of place in the barren landscape.

The next eight miles of the road past Last Chance Creek are slow going as it winds into and out of many small canyons and washes. The road straightens just after passing Ship Mountain Point, the giant stone monolith that looms high above the surroundings.

Ship Mountain Point

Just south of Ship Mountain Point, Heads of the Creek Road branches off to the right. This road provides access to some interesting canyons in the Dirty Devil area. A sign along Heads of the Creek Road indicates that a number of traps have been set for dangerous animals and that a sharp eye should be kept on children and pets while in the area.

Smoky Hollow Canyon Road is off Smoky Mountain Road three miles south of the junction with Heads of the Creek Road. Smoky Hollow Canyon Road is an alternate way off the plateau and is a fairly good road. Smoky Hollow is a very colorful canyon that consists of oxidized red-colored sandstone, green-and-yellowish shale, and black coal. The canyon was the location of the proposed coal mine on the plateau (*see* Coal Mines on the Kaiparowits? on page 76). The only road that turns off Smoky Hollow Canyon Road is Tibbet Canyon Road, about two miles before Smoky Hollow Canyon Road reconnects with Smoky Mountain Road.

Past the junction with Smoky Hollow Canyon Road, Smoky Mountain Road takes a relatively straight course across Smoky Mountain, which is famous for its underground burning coal beds (25). At times the smoke from these fires can be seen from the road.

Smoky Mountain Road abruptly drops off of Smoky Mountain and descends almost one thousand feet to the flats near Lake Powell. This steep decline is known as Kelly Grade. The steep switchbacks of Kelly Grade are quite intimidating and have sheer drop-offs on one side of the small dirt road and cliffs on the other. This section of the road provides amazing views of the badlands at the base of the plateau and views of Lake Powell and Navajo Mountain in the distance.

The road from the bottom of Kelly Grade to the town of Big Water travels through a barren moonscape of rocky cliffs and multicolored badlands. Rounded domes of shale surround the road, often taking on strange shapes and forms. The colors of the hills and knolls range from creamy whites to almost stark blacks, creating an almost unnatural scene. This feeling is enhanced by the lack of plant life, which is a result of soil acidity. This portion of the road is quick driving and well graded.

Coal Canyon (22)

Overview

Coal Canyon is one of the most accessible canyons of the Kaiparowits Plateau. It is similar to many of the canyons that drain the plateau and is a good one to visit to get a general feel of the area. This canyon offers easy hiking and a chance to see some unusual rocks.

Access

Coal Canyon is located four and a half miles south of Escalante on Smoky Mountain Road, which enters Alvey Wash about two miles south of Escalante. Coal Canyon is the first large wash to enter Alvey Wash from the right. This section of the road is well graded, but where it crosses Coal Canyon, Smoky Mountain Road becomes quite sandy and rutted (this is a good landmark). It is possible to drive up Coal Canyon for a short distance.

Difficulty

Hiking up the smooth bottom of Coal Canyon is quite easy. The broad canyon bottom makes a good mountain-bike trail.

Maps

1:100,000 Escalante
1:24,000 Canaan Creek

Elevation

Top: 6,660 feet
Bottom: 6,160 feet

Water

It is best to bring your own.

Camping

Primitive car camping is available at the mouth of Coal Canyon or at Camp Flat (24). The closest established campground is at the Escalante Petrified Forest State Park (8).

Route Description

The walls of Coal Canyon come down in a staircase-like pattern rather than as sheer cliffs. This pattern results from the more-resistant sandstone layers forming small cliffs and the less-resistant coal and shale layers forming the gradual sloping parts of the canyon walls.

The walls of Coal Canyon that have a southern exposure are lined with pinyon-juniper forests, and those with a northern exposure have ponderosa pine trees in addition to these forests. A few cottonwood trees grow in Coal Canyon's gravelly wash.

Clinkers, rocks associated with coal beds that have burned underground, can be found in the wash. Look along the gravel banks and sandbars. Clinkers are typically red or black in color.

Mitchell Canyon branches off to the right a mile from the mouth of Coal Canyon. An old jeep trail runs up the bottom of Mitchell Canyon, which is rockier and a bit narrower than Coal Canyon. Even though Coal Canyon is easier walking, Mitchell Canyon is the more interesting route.

Trap Canyon (23)

Overview

Trap Canyon is a remote and unusually narrow canyon in the heart of the Kaiparowits Plateau. Hanging gardens, cedars, and Douglas fir are all found within the canyon's confines. The road to Trap Canyon goes over Death Ridge and offers superb views of the plateau region.

Access

Head south out of the town of Escalante on Smoky Mountain Road. Take a right on the road leading to Death Ridge at the first marked junction on Smoky Mountain Road, eight miles south of Escalante. Death Ridge is six miles from this junction along a good dirt road. Upon arriving at the top of Death Ridge, there will be good views of the Kaiparowits Plateau, Henry Mountains, and Boulder Mountain. Death Ridge received its name when a herd of cattle was marooned in a snowstorm and died along the ridge top. Continue driving along the ridge for two miles before taking a left onto the only decent road in the vicinity. (If you miss this left, Death Ridge Road immediately begins to deteriorate and ends altogether in another mile or so.) From the left-hand turnoff of Death Ridge Road, it is another mile down a steep and bumpy road to Trap

Trap Canyon

Canyon. After this steep decline, Trap Canyon is the first wash you will encounter. Past Trap Canyon, a four-wheel-drive road continues toward Paradise Canyon (29).

Difficulty

There is easy hiking in the wash, and no obstacles are found within the narrows of Trap Canyon. The first three miles down the canyon from the road are very narrow and scenic. After about three miles, the canyon begins to gradually widen.

Map

1:24,000 Death Ridge

Elevation

7,100 feet to 6,800 feet

Water

It is best to bring your own water.

Camping

There is good car camping near the end of Death Ridge Road. This area is referred to as Lonesome Pine Flat on the Death Ridge Quad.

Route Description

Early ranchers used Trap Canyon as a holding area for livestock and horses. The narrow walls of Trap Canyon made closing off the canyon essential, creating a trap for livestock. During the spring, the canyon could hold as many as twelve horses for thirty days.

Trap Canyon is somewhat unique due to its beautiful section of narrows, a rare find on the Kaiparowits Plateau. When I hiked this canyon there were no other signs of human visitors. If you have entered the right canyon, you will encounter a dry waterfall an eighth of a mile from the road. This dry-fall is easily negotiated. The canyon then becomes quite narrow (four to eight feet) for the next half mile.

The high elevation and shade provided by the canyon walls make the canyon an oasis for plant life. Douglas fir (uncommon elsewhere on the plateau) ponderosa pine, oak, wild roses, and cedar all grow along the wash. (Cedars are quite different from junipers because they require more water; they have flat leaves, different berries, slightly different bark, and can grow much larger.) Hanging gardens occupy the small holes and rock crevices of the narrows. Many tracks of deer and other smaller wildlife can be seen on the wash floor.

The canyon remains narrow for three miles, with beautiful trees and scenery, before it begins to gradually open up. Ponderosa pine and Douglas fir have fallen across the narrow wash in a number of places.

Camp Flat (24)

A favorite camping site of early day ranchers, Camp Flat is an excellent site for car camping adjacent to Smoky Mountain Road. Camp Flat makes a good base camp (tent or trailer) for exploring the many canyons in the area, such as Carcass and Sarah Ann Canyons. Camp Flat is located along Smoky Mountain Road, five miles south of the Death Ridge turnoff (thirteen miles south of Escalante). Camp Flat is a well-used campsite located on the flats right after the road comes up the steep grade at the end of Alvey Wash.

It is very easy to reach the rim of the Straight Cliffs from Camp Flat. Excellent views of the canyons of the Escalante are obtained from the top of these cliffs. To reach the rim, head east from Camp Flat on a four-wheel-drive road. Take a left at the first junction after about three-quarters of a mile and drive in a northeasterly direction for another two miles or until the road is no longer driveable. Then park and walk due east about a mile to the edge of the Straight Cliffs. When following this route it helps to have the appropriate 1:24,000 quad.

Smoky Mountain Burning Coal Beds (25)

The Smoky Mountain Burning Coal Beds are one of the most novel sites along Smoky Mountain Road. Underneath the Kaiparowits Plateau, giant coal deposits have been burning for thousands of years. Most of these fires were started by lightning that struck areas where the coal is exposed at the surface. Some of the smoke from

Smoky Mountain Burning Coal Beds

these underground fires rises to the surface through vents near Smoky Mountain Road.

To reach the Burning Coal Beds, drive south on Smoky Mountain Road four miles past the marked junction with Smoky Mountain Hollow Road. The turnoff to the coal beds is on the east side of the road and is shaped like a Y. It is the only turnoff of this nature in the area. Alternately, those traveling northward from Big Water should drive about two miles past the top of the Kelly Grade to this turnoff.

Once you are on the small road leading to the Burning Coal Beds, proceed about a mile and they should come into view. On most days these steaming vents will be visible from Smoky Mountain Road, so locating them should not be difficult.

The dozen or so vents are not extremely deep and several small beds of coal can be seen in the vicinity. The smoke and water vapor pouring out of these strange vents is very sulfuric and noxious, and the openings seem quite at home in this barren landscape.

HOLE-IN-THE-ROCK ROAD: ROUTE DESCRIPTION

This fifty-seven-mile-long, graded dirt road travels to the Hole-in-the-Rock where in 1880 Mormon settlers engineered a passage for their wagons down a 1,200-foot cliff to get to the bottom of the Colorado River Canyon. Hole-in-the-Rock Road heads south from Highway 12, five miles east of Escalante. The road provides access to the Straight Cliffs, the Kaiparowits Plateau, and a number of Escalante River side canyons.

When you travel down Hole-in-the-Rock Road, you will pass numerous features with names like Ten-Mile Wash and Twenty-Mile Bench. Today, with our rapid rates of travel, the names seem almost meaningless; but to the early ranchers traveling on horseback, they were more significant. The mileages are all in reference to the distance from Escalante, and the names served almost as a street map for the early cowboys. Looking at the names from that perspective, it makes more sense that the wash located halfway between Ten- and Twenty-Mile Wash is called Halfway Hollow. Not all of the names are drab; for instance, the Sooner Road was named after a sheepherder who said, "I'd sooner be home than here."

Most of Hole-in-the-Rock Road is in good condition, but the last eight miles of the road require a four-wheel-drive vehicle. The road is impassable during periods of bad weather.

Hole-in-the-Rock Road traverses the large flat benches at the base of the Straight Cliffs, which are the eastern boundary of the Kaiparowits Plateau. These cliffs are over a thousand feet tall and run from north to south for fifty miles; hence, they are commonly referred to as Fiftymile Mountain. The Straight Cliffs are breached by only one four-wheel-drive road in their fifty-mile length. This road connects Hole-in-the-Rock Road to Smoky Mountain Road.

On the east side of the road lie the canyons of the Escalante River, and Hole-in-the-Rock Road provides access to many of its tributaries. Many of these scenic side canyons are within the boundaries of Glen Canyon National Recreation Area, and information about hiking them can be obtained from the interagency visitor's center in Escalante. Views of these scenic canyons are limited from Hole-in-

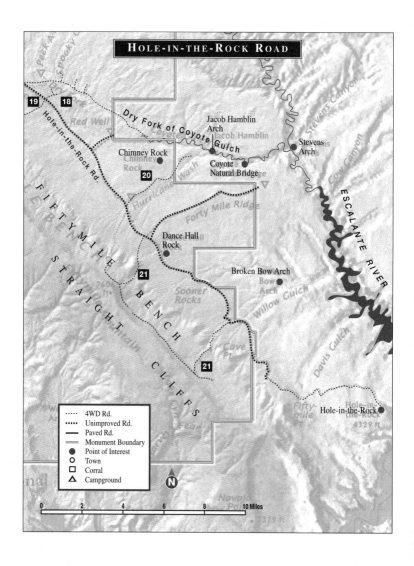

HOLE-IN-THE-ROCK ROAD

the-Rock Road, but most of the broad washes that cross this road eventually turn into deep and convoluted canyons.

The Hole-in-the-Rock Story

Two-hundred and fifty Mormon pioneers, including women and children, first traveled the Hole-in-the-Rock route in 1880. Church leaders had requested that this group of pioneers settle in the Four Corners area, near the San Juan River.

The Hole-in-the-Rock route was chosen because it was the most direct route. Little was known about the difficulties that would be encountered. The pioneers had prepared for a six-week journey that ended up lasting six months.

They spent weeks camping near Dance Hall Rock while they worked on blasting out a wagon route down the steep cliffs of the Colorado River Canyon. A route was constructed and the pioneers built a barge to ferry the wagons across the river. Not a single wagon was lost on the descent.

After crossing the river, a rough route lay ahead through sandstone canyons and ridges. The pioneers became so worn out and tired that they stopped eighteen miles from their final destination and founded the town of Bluff.

Cedar Wash Arch (15)

This beautiful arch is formed into the cream-colored sandstones of Cedar Wash. To get to the arch, drive four miles south on Hole-in-the-Rock Road from Highway 12 to Cedar Wash Road, which takes off on the right side of Hole-in-the-Rock Road just before crossing Alvey Wash. The wash is marked by a sign but Cedar Wash Road is not. Travel west along Cedar Wash Road for about three miles and park at a pull-off on the left side of the road. The road makes a sharp bend to the right at the parking area. Walk south from the road a fifth of a mile to the sandstone cliffs overlooking Cedar Wash, and the arch can be seen downstream along the sandstone cliffs on the left side of the wash. It is not necessary to descend all the way to the canyon floor to see it. Cedar Wash Arch has evolved into Dakota Sandstone, which is a creamy-white color that becomes

Cedar Wash Arch

quite rounded and smooth where it is exposed. This sandstone formation of ancient beach deposit is only fifty to a hundred feet thick.

Devils Garden (16)

This area of oddly shaped rocks at the base of the Straight Cliffs is a good place for a picnic lunch. Devils Garden is twelve miles down Hole-in-the-Rock Road from Highway 12 and then a half mile to the east on a marked road. Tables, fire pits, and rest rooms are available, and footpaths lead through the strange and unique rock formations.

The balanced rocks, strangely shaped pillars, and arches of Devils Garden all formed as a result of differential erosion, which occurs because harder more-resistant rocks erode at a slower rate than weaker less-resistant rocks. Examples of differential erosion can be seen anyplace hard rocks and soft rocks are found side by side. The harder rocks will always express themselves better, and weaker rocks will stand lower and recede below the harder rocks. In Devils

Devils Garden

Garden, for instance, the balanced rocks are more resistant to erosion than the rock that supports them.

Left Hand of Collet Canyon (17)

Overview

A four-wheel-drive route runs through this deep canyon and connects Hole-in-the-Rock Road with Smoky Mountain Road (*see* Smoky Mountain Road on page 78). Visible coal seams can be seen in this fairly narrow canyon, and an extensive network of side canyons provides a good opportunity for exploration.

Access

Travel south thirteen miles on Hole-in-the-Rock Road from Highway 12 and take a right at the sign indicating Collet Canyon. The road heads toward the Straight Cliffs and does not enter Collet Canyon for about five miles. Sections of the road between the canyon entrance and Hole-in-the-Rock Road are quite sandy.

Driving up Collet Canyon is only possible in a high-clearance, four-wheel-drive vehicle. When I drove the road in April, thick areas of mud had developed in places where the creek ran along the road. Up the canyon, the road gradually improved as the wash bottom gradually become sandier and more gravelly. If the road up Collet Canyon is impassable, it may still be possible to drive the first five miles to the mouth of the canyon and hike up the wash.

Difficulty

Walking along the bottom of the wash is quite easy and no serious obstacles are present. The Left Hand of Collet Canyon is about five miles long, and the road runs through the canyon for three of the five miles.

Map

1:24,000 Seep Flat

Elevation

5,400 feet to 6,000 feet

Left Hand of Collet Canyon

Water

Water only runs seasonally through the Left Hand of Collet Canyon and its various side canyons.

Camping

Good car camping is possible near Collet Top Junction and near the Dry Fork of Coyote Gulch along Hole-in-the-Rock Road.

Route Description

The Left Hand of Collet Canyon is almost 800 feet deep. The canyon walls descend in a staircase-like pattern rather than in sheer cliffs. Layers of coal, present in the canyon walls, are difficult to see because they are often covered by a mantle of debris that has crept and slumped downhill from overlying shale and sandstone layers. The best place to see exposed layers of coal is in the wash of Collet Canyon, upstream from the junction with Lower Trail Canyon.

Willard Canyon enters the Left Hand of Collet Canyon from the right, about three miles upstream from the mouth of the Left Hand of Collet Canyon at the base of the Straight Cliffs. A balanced rock that is quite distinctive is seen just before the mouth of Willard Canyon. An old corral is visible a fifth of a mile up the canyon, and small nodules of iron and pyrite can be found farther on.

Just a short distance past the mouth of Willard Canyon, the road leaves the Left Hand of Collet Canyon (it continues up Lower Trail Canyon to Collet Junction). Some of the best hiking in Collet Canyon is found upstream from where the road leaves the canyon. It is here that the Left Hand of Collet Canyon begins to widen and the wash divides into numerous smaller washes; this is a good place to turn around.

Batty Pass Caves (19)

These caves were blasted out of sheer sandstone cliffs and were lived in by two local rock hounds/craftsmen during the 1950s for four or five years. The caves are reached by driving twenty-one miles down Hole-in-the-Rock Road to the four-way junction marked on the left side of the road going to the Dry Fork of Coyote Gulch Trailhead. Take a right at this four-way junction, even though a sign indicates this as a dead-end road, and drive two and a half miles to the caves. The road crosses a number of washes that require a high-clearance vehicle. At the caves, the road all but ends, leaving only a faint track. Just before you reach the caves, you will see a rusted-out car on the left side of the road.

Bill and Cliff Lichtenhahn—who cut and polished petrified wood and jasper to build tabletops, checkerboards, and such—were the craftsmen who lived in the Batty Pass Caves. These men explored the desert canyons and the Straight Cliffs, looking for suitable rocks. A number of power tools were employed by the men to aid in their building efforts and in their work as craftsmen. Referred to by locals as "the cavemen," they visited the town of Escalante about once a week to gather supplies and sell their goods. Of the three caves, two were used as workshops and one as living quarters. Today, the caves contain the remains of old beds and shelves.

Dry Fork of Coyote Gulch (18)

Overview

Some of the Southwest's narrowest slot canyons are found in the Dry Fork of Coyote Gulch. These canyons are so narrow that it is necessary to walk sideways and even crawl in a few places. The slot canyons are easily reached and are one of the more popular sites along Hole-in-the-Rock Road.

Access

Drive twenty-one miles south on Hole-in-the-Rock Road and take a left on the marker road leading to the Dry Fork of Coyote Gulch. Drive another three-quarters of a mile to a small junction. Take a left at this junction and drive another mile to the official trailhead.

Difficulty

Hiking through the slot canyons is moderately difficult. Do not carry excess gear through the canyons because they are so narrow that it will not fit. Even a small backpack can be cumbersome. Hiking through all the narrow side canyons and back to the trailhead is a seven-mile round-trip.

Map

1:24,000 Big Hollow Wash

Elevation

Top: 6,600 feet
Bottom: 4,600 feet

Water

These washes and canyons are usually dry.

Camping

Some good car camping exists along the dirt roads.

Route Description

From the trailhead, follow the path northwest for half a mile along the rim overlooking the canyon. When possible, descend from the ridge and follow one of the washes down to the narrows of the Dry Fork of Coyote Gulch. These narrows are about a half mile in length. They open up very close to the mouth of Peek-a-boo Canyon, but where Peek-a-boo enters is difficult to spot because it is a very small opening in the sandstone walls above an eight-foot dry-fall.

The easiest route is to go up Spooky Canyon and down Peek-a-boo. To find Spooky Canyon, walk downstream from the end of the narrows of the Dry Fork of Coyote Gulch for a half mile to where a trail goes up Spooky Canyon. I missed this trail on the my first trip and found that by walking down the Dry Fork of Coyote Gulch just a little bit farther it is possible to walk directly up Spooky Canyon from its intersection with the Dry Fork of Coyote Gulch.

Spooky Canyon gets really narrow, and in some places it is only ten to twelve inches wide. Needless to say, do not bring a lot of gear into the canyon. The narrows of Spooky Canyon are less than a mile long. Upon exiting the narrows, look to the left to find a trail going up over a sand dune that leads to Peek-a-boo Canyon. It is a short walk to the canyon, and rock cairns have been placed along the route. Peek-a-boo is not as narrow as Spooky, but it has an interesting double arch.

Another narrow side canyon of the Dry Fork of Coyote Gulch is Brimstone Gulch, a mile and a half downstream from the intersection of the Dry Fork of Coyote Gulch and Spooky Canyon. Before arriving at Brimstone Gulch, you will encounter another set of narrows containing one choke stone I had difficulty getting my dog around, but it is easily passable for hikers. Brimstone is the first side canyon on the left after this section of narrows, and it begins as a broad sandy wash. Walk up Brimstone Gulch for three-quarters of a mile to the narrows. These were my favorite narrows in the area, as they seemed very deep and dark although not as narrow as Spooky. Some deep pools blocked further progress about a half mile from the start of the narrows.

Chimney Rock (20)

This rock spire jutting out from the flats of the Escalante desert seems to almost defy erosion. The spire is located thirty-two and a half miles down Hole-in-the-Rock Road from Highway 12. The road takes off Hole-in-the-Rock Road on the east side and is marked by a sign.

Chimney Rock was an important landmark to early travelers. As its name implies, the rock spire looks much like a giant stovepipe. It is unclear if Chimney Rock is the erosional remnant of an ancient mesa or if its origin is similar to the rock spires of Kodachrome Basin (31). If it is a feature formed by erosion, it would be properly termed a "monument."

Fiftymile Bench (21)

To reach Fiftymile Bench, drive forty-five miles south on Hole-in-the-Rock Road and take a right at a well-marked junction. The road leading up to Fiftymile Bench is very steep and consists of big ruts and rocks. A jeep or four-wheeler can drive up this road, or it makes a good hiking route. The road offers good views of Boulder Mountain, the Escalante Basin, and the Straight Cliffs.

An easier route to the top of Fiftymile Bench is via Sooner Bench Road, a fairly good road that was initially built to go to the top of the Kaiparowits Plateau. Some of the best views of the entire area are from the top of Fiftymile Bench.

Window Wind Arch is found at the very top and edge of the Straight Cliffs. It is reached by hiking up an old cattle trail at the north end of Fiftymile Bench to the top of the Kaiparowits Plateau. From Hole-in-the-Rock Road, take a right at the sign indicating Fiftymile Bench. Drive up the steep road to the top and take a right onto a small four-wheel-drive route. The old cattle trail switchbacking up to the top of the Kaiparowits Plateau should be visible. Since it is a steep hike to the top of the plateau, drive as close as possible to the trail before you begin hiking toward it. Window Wind Arch is about a half mile north along the rim of the plateau from where the trail reaches the top. The old cattle ranchers I talked to indicated that the Indians used the trail to the top of the Kaiparowits long before ranching began in the area. Ranchers moved as many as 350 cattle up and down this trail every year.

The names of numerous cattle ranchers have been inscribed on the walls of Window Wind Arch. One name of particular interest is that of "Lewollen Harris 1888." Harris was an eccentric Mormon missionary/explorer and one of the first white men to explore the area. Harris was looking for the Golden Image (an image of the Savior made from gold) supposedly hidden on Fiftymile Mountain. Harris had a rough map of the location of the Golden Image but was unable to find it.

CROTON/GRAND BENCH ROAD:
ROUTE DESCRIPTION

Croton Road follows a series of knife-edge ridges across the Kaiparowits Plateau before making a steep decline to the benchland above Lake Powell. These ridges offer views of the Burning Hills, the area called "East of the Navajos," Navajo Canyon, the back side of the Straight Cliffs, and Lake Powell.

This is one of the least-accessible roads in the monument and should only be attempted by a high-clearance, four-wheel-drive during good weather. Croton Road is sixty-nine miles long, and when I drove the road in my Land Cruiser, it took over eight hours. Much of this time I spent making road repairs, as recent rains had made deep ruts that needed to be filled in with rocks. Make sure to take enough gas, water, and food so that the necessary supplies will be at hand if your vehicle breaks down.

Croton Road is accessed via Smoky Mountain Road. Drive twenty-seven miles south of Escalante along Smoky Mountain Road and take a left toward Collet Top Junction. This left turn is not easily missed because a cattleman's cabin and corral sit right at the intersection. Turn left at the cabin and drive another three miles to Collet Top Junction. Croton Road takes off to the right from here. This right turn is indicated by a sign marked "Big Water 69 miles." Head south on Croton Road toward Big Water, drive another eight miles, and take a right at the sign indicating "Big Water 61 miles." If you miss this last turn, you will encounter a large exploratory oil well within three miles. When I approached the oil well, two Kane County police officers stopped me and would not let me proceed past the oil well to the area called "East of the Navajos."

Croton Road continues south along the tops of a series of sparsely vegetated ridges. Deep canyons lie to either side of the ridges, and views of distant mountains and mesas can be seen in all directions. The blue waters of Lake Powell seem to appear almost out of nowhere. This giant lake sits in stark contrast to the barren landscape. The Burning Hills (26) are seen to the west before the road descends to Grand Bench.

Croton Road makes a steep descent off the Kaiparowits Plateau to the flats above Lake Powell where it connects with Grand Bench Road. After descending off the plateau, take a right where Croton Road comes to a T with Grand Bench Road. This is the only intersection within miles, and, although unmarked, it is fairly obvious.

Grand Bench Road heads east around the ridges and in and out of the washes extending from the Kaiparowits Plateau. It is twenty miles from the intersection of Croton Road and Grand Bench Road to Smoky Mountain Road. Deep washes, multicolored shale badlands, and intricately weathered sandstone knobs and buttes dominate the landscape. The giant eroding mesas that form the south end of the Kaiparowits Plateau are one of the most impressive features on this drive. The colors of these mesas are a dramatic mix of reds, blacks, and grays.

Burning Hills (26)

The Burning Hills are best seen from Croton Road before it descends to the flats above Lake Powell. The hills have a distinctive red coloring that is a result of oxidation created by underground coal fires that have been burning for hundreds of years; in places, smoke can be seen rising from the ground. Claims are made that vents similar to the Burning Coal Beds of Smoky Mountain (25) exist in the Burning Hills. Many of the coal beds of the plateau have caught fire at one time or another, resulting in destruction of about 30 percent of all the coal on the plateau.

The rugged topography of the area and generally bad roads keep most people away from the Burning Hills. Hikers and backpackers who want to explore the area are sure to find solitude. The canyons in the area are dry for the most part, so bring plenty of water.

FOUR MILE BENCH ROAD: ROUTE DESCRIPTION

Four Mile Bench Road provides access to Grosvenor Arch and the northwest corner of the Kaiparowits Plateau. Some of the canyons that cut into Four Mile Bench make for excellent hiking. The relatively flat and rolling terrain of Four Mile Bench provides an ideal habitat for juniper and pinyon pine trees; some of these trees are from 1,200 to 1,800 years old.

Four Mile Bench Road is reached by taking Cottonwood Wash Road south from the town of Cannonville. Follow the road for eighteen miles and take a left at the marked turnoff to Grosvenor Arch. Located on Four Mile Bench Road, Grosvenor Arch (27) is only a one-mile drive off Cottonwood Wash Road. Four Mile Bench Road is a fairly good dirt road, passable to all types of vehicles.

Continue east on Four Mile Bench Road past Grosvenor Arch, and the road will cross over the double-ridged spine of the Cockscomb. The top of the Cockscomb offers great views of the Kaiparowits Plateau, and the spine of the Cockscomb can be seen stretching off into the distance. Traveling east across Four Mile Bench, the road crosses Wahweap Creek, Blue Wash, Tommy Creek, Half-Mile Wash, and Four Mile Canyon.

Grosvenor Arch (27)

This light-colored, spectacular double arch is formed in Dakota Sandstone. The top of the arch is 152 feet off the ground and it is 92 feet wide. This arch is just a mile's drive off of Cottonwood Wash Road on Four Mile Bench Road.

The arch was formerly considered part of Kodachrome Basin State Park but now lies within the monument's boundaries. Originally called Butler Arch, it was renamed in 1949 by the National Geographic Society after a former president of the society.

A no-fee primitive campground with tables and fire pits is found near the base of the arch. Sites are limited at this campground, but there is enough room for one large group.

Grosvenor Arch

Tommy Canyon (28)

Overview

Unlike many of the canyons of the Kaiparowits Plateau, Tommy Canyon has a small year-round stream. The canyon walls are host to numerous overhangs and small caves. Large alcoves, side canyons, cottonwood trees, and desert springs adorned with hanging gardens make this an interesting hike.

Access

Tommy Canyon is located five and a half miles east of Grosvenor Arch along Four Mile Bench Road. Before reaching Tommy Canyon, Four Mile Bench Road crosses Wahweap and Blue Washes, both marked by signs. The road to Tommy Canyon takes off to the left about a mile and a half after crossing Blue Wash. The road is unmarked but has a distinctive Y-type junction. Drive a mile down this road to where it ends in the wash near an old fence and corral.

Difficulty

Many of the stream terraces are laced with old cow and deer trails, which make hiking easy. The creek is small enough that it can be easily jumped across in most places. It is about two miles to the junction with Half-Mile Canyon and four miles to the junction with Four Mile Canyon.

Maps

1:24,000 Horse Mountain
1:24,000 Four Mile Bench

Elevation

5,600 feet to 5,300 feet

Water

Water runs continuously in Tommy Canyon; however, the area is used for grazing, so all water should be treated.

Camping

There are good places for car camping on Four Mile Bench and established campgrounds at Grosvenor Arch and Kodachrome Basin State Park.

Route Description

Tommy Canyon begins as a broad wash with almost nonexistent canyon walls. Downstream, the cliff walls gradually rise and the canyon narrows. The yearlong flow of water in the canyon leads to areas of thick vegetation. Cottonwood trees, willows, and tamarisks fill the wash while pinyon pine and juniper trees grow along the benches and cliff terraces.

The buff-colored sandstone walls of the canyon are beset with small caves, and most of them are occupied by birds' nests. Large alcoves, numerous overhangs, and the presence of perpetual water make this canyon a potentially good prospect to find Anasazi and Fremont ruins.

ATV (all-terrain-vehicle) tracks are sometimes present in the bottom of the wash. These tracks are probably made by ranchers who use ATVs to round up cattle. A small rancher's cabin can be seen on a ridge on the right side of the wash about a half mile down the canyon from the end of the road.

Half-Mile Canyon enters Tommy Canyon on the left after about two miles. A large rock pedestal marks the mouth of Half-Mile Canyon, a deep canyon filled with giant cottonwood trees. An abandoned meander of Tommy Canyon is present at the mouth of Half-Mile Canyon.

Four Mile Canyon enters Tommy Canyon on the left about four miles downstream from the car park. It is possible to hike back to Four Mile Bench Road via Four Mile Canyon, but taking this route requires leaving a car on Four Mile Bench Road at the head of Four Mile Canyon.

Paradise Canyon (29)

Overview

This is a deep canyon in the middle of the Kaiparowits Plateau. This remote and isolated canyon has a year-round stream, an unusual feature on the arid Kaiparowits Plateau. Giant cottonwood trees and fairly thick streamside vegetation exist here. Rock pinnacles, giant alcoves that descend to the canyon floor, desert springs, good camping, and hanging gardens make this little canyon an oasis atop the plateau.

Access

Travel east on Four Mile Bench eleven miles past Grosvenor Arch. Take a left turn at a signed junction indicating "Paradise Canyon Junction 2 miles." Continue two miles to the junction, which is easily missed as only a small road takes off to the left. Take a right at Paradise Canyon Junction and drive another mile and a half to where the road ends in the side canyon of Paradise Canyon. Park either at the end of the road or drive down the wash a little way toward Paradise Canyon, which is another two miles. The roads to Paradise Canyon are quite well maintained and can be managed by most passenger cars.

Difficulty

Walking in the bottom of Paradise Canyon is easy although no trail exists, and the small stream is easily crossed without getting your feet wet. Paradise Canyon is roughly fifteen miles long, but the route described below only covers five of the fifteen miles.

Paradise Canyon

Map
1:24,000 Horse Mountain

Elevation
Top: 6,600 feet
Bottom: 5,560 feet

Water
Water flows year round in Paradise Canyon; however, cattle graze in the canyon, so treat water carefully.

Camping
There is good car camping near Paradise Canyon Junction. Established campgrounds exist at Grosvenor Arch and Kodachrome Basin State Park.

Route Description
This route begins at one of Paradise Canyon's side canyons, which gradually deepens until its intersection with Paradise Canyon (about a mile and a half). Some springs are located about a half mile from where the road ends, and water is present in the canyon the rest of the way down to the junction with Paradise Canyon.

A grove of cottonwood trees is present at the Paradise Canyon junction. A flat sandy area beneath the trees makes a good place for camping or picnicking.

Paradise Canyon starts as a broad but deep canyon. The canyon walls are made up of sandstone ledges and intervening talus slopes. The sandstone walls are painted with a dark desert varnish, and numerous water pockets have developed.

Upstream, the canyon goes through a series of meanders for about two miles before it gradually begins to narrow. Cottonwoods and willows line the bank, and the canyon bottom is a lush green color in the spring. Some of the alcoves even have seeps that support hanging gardens.

Two other possible access routes to the upper stretches of Paradise Canyon exist. The first of these continues north from Paradise Canyon Junction, and the second is from Trap Canyon (23).

4

White Cliffs

The Grand Staircase/Paria River Country

Overview

At the same time the first modern expedition was gearing up to explore Utah's Grand Staircase, tourists were feeding the bears along the highways in Yellowstone National Park. This exploratory expedition, funded by the National Geographic Society, consisted of three jeeps, two trucks, and thirty-five horses. In 1949, the expedition headed off into one of the least-known wilderness areas in the United States.

The expedition roughly followed the route now taken by Cotton-wood Wash Road. They captured the first images of Grosvenor Arch on film and named it after the president of the National Geographic Society. The name Kodachrome was given to the area around Kodachrome State Park. Local ranchers originally called this area Thorny Pasture. Expedition leaders generalized the area as being an "agricultural wasteland . . . , but for the geologist or explorer who likes to get as far off the beaten track as possible it is a paradise."

Numerous canyons cut the cliffs of the Grand Staircase, resulting in their broken and rugged profile (*see* Geology of the Monument on page 21). The subtle and discontinuous cliffs of the Grand Staircase are not as easily recognized as the Straight Cliffs, whose continuous rampart can be seen for miles. The Grand Staircase is such a large feature that it can be difficult to recognize individual cliffs as part of it. The best views of the cliffs of the Grand Staircase are from the southern half of the monument, along Highway 89 and Nipple Ranch Road.

The Paria River and its many tributaries cut through the cliffs of the Grand Staircase and form magnificent steep-walled canyons. The Vermilion Cliffs' canyons host giant alcoves, amphitheaters, hanging gardens, and Anasazi Ruins and are usually wider than the canyons of the White Cliffs. Because they are higher in elevation than the Vermilion Cliffs, the White Cliffs' canyons have more water and more vegetation. The Navajo Sandstone that forms the cliffs has a tendency to erode into deep, narrow slot canyons.

The Grand Staircase is bounded on the west by the rim of Bryce Canyon, to the east by the Cockscomb (a fold in the earth's crust), to the north by the Aquarius Plateau, and to the south by the Colorado River. The Paria River, within the boundaries of the monument, cuts through both the White and Vermilion Cliffs of the Grand Staircase.

The area of the Grand Staircase/Paria River drainage is essentially one large wilderness area. Few good roads exist, and the four-wheel-drive roads that do reach into the backcountry are so rough that they are seldom used. Designation of the Grand Staircase as part of a national monument will, hopefully, help to preserve its unique wilderness character. The Grand Staircase has not changed significantly since that National Geographic expedition in 1949, and it still remains a mecca for adventurers who want to get off the beaten track.

Access to the Paria River and Grand Staircase

Getting to the canyons and mesas of the Grand Staircase is mainly via one of four routes: Skutumpah Road on the west side, Highway 12 to the north, Cottonwood Wash Road on the east, and Highway 89 along the south end. Of these roads, Skutumpah Road and Cottonwood Wash Road are not paved. These four roads form a box in which a great area of wildlands is enclosed.

HIGHWAY 12: THE BLUES (30)

The area of Badlands known as the Blues lies about fifteen miles east of Tropic on Highway 12. In this area, Tropic shale has weathered into barren hills and intricate drainage patterns. The shale was

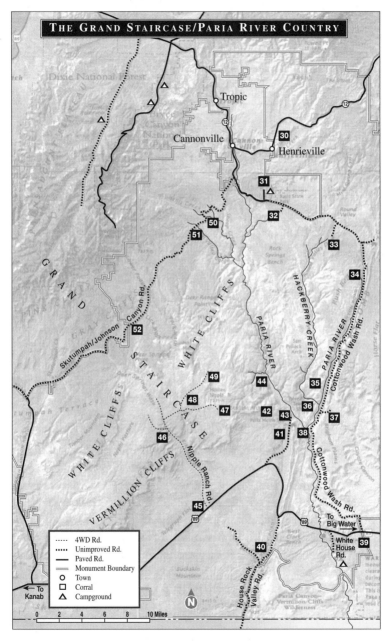

THE GRAND STAIRCASE/PARIA RIVER COUNTRY

Dixie National Forest

Tropic

Cannonville

Henrieville

30

31

32

33

34

50

51

52

GRAND

WHITE CLIFFS

STAIRCASE

HACKBERRY CREEK

PARIA RIVER

Skutumpah/Johnson Canyon Rd.

Cottonwood Wash Rd.

49

48

47

46

44

42

43

41

35

36

37

38

Nipple Ranch Rd.

WHITE CLIFFS

VERMILLION CLIFFS

45

89

89

40

39

To Big Water

White House Rd.

House Rock Valley Rd.

Cottonwood Wash Rd.

Paria Canyon-Vermilion Cliffs Wilderness

4WD Rd.
Unimproved Rd.
Paved Rd.
Monument Boundary
O   Town
□   Corral
△   Campground

To Kanab

0   2   4   6   8   10 Miles

N

deposited about eighty million years ago during the Cretaceous period, when Utah was covered by a large ocean. As a result, Tropic shale is a good place to look for marine fossils, particularly oysters and mollusks.

This shale is seen farther to the northwest around the base of the Henry Mountains and near Cainsville where it goes by the name of Mancos shale. Different names, but it is essentially the same rock deposited in the same environment.

One of the best options for exploring the Blues is to drive the jeep trail up Henderson Creek. This trail is accessed from the town of Tropic.

Cottonwood Wash Road: Route Description

One of the most enjoyable and scenic drives in the monument is on Cottonwood Wash Road. This road is used to access the upper Paria River, Grosvenor Arch, areas of the Kaiparowits Plateau, and the Cockscomb. The route was first improved for passenger vehicles in 1957. Local citizens paid for improvements with hopes that it would become the major route from northern Utah to the Glen Canyon Dam. Most of the road is unpaved, and its clayish surface becomes impassable when wet. No services are available along this forty-six-mile stretch of road between Highway 12 and Highway 89. To drive the entire forty-six miles takes a little over two and a half hours.

Cottonwood Wash Road heads south from the town of Cannonville, located along Highway 12, where it parallels and then crosses the Paria River. Just before crossing the river, four miles south of Cannonville, the Skutumpah-Bull Valley Gorge Road takes off on the right side of Cottonwood Wash Road *(see* Skutumpah Road description on page 151). The Paria is a small muddy stream most of the time, but during periods of runoff it can be a raging torrent. The road is paved for the first nine miles between Cannonville and the turnoff to Kodachrome Basin State Park (31); the state park offers the only developed campground in the area.

From the turnoff to Kodachrome Basin State Park (31), Cottonwood Wash Road continues east. The road traverses a broad valley that is host to brilliantly colored cliffs and intricately eroded rock forms. The road crosses Rock Springs Creek (32), Hackberry Canyon (36), and Round Valley Draw (33) before the turnoff to Grosvenor Arch is encountered, seven miles past Kodachrome Basin State Park. Grosvenor Arch (27), one of the largest double arches in the world, is located on the Four Mile Bench Road (*see* description on page 104), just a mile off Cottonwood Wash Road.

Past the junction with Four Mile Bench, Cottonwood Wash Road makes a sharp turn south and parallels the Cockscomb (37), which is a giant fold in the earth's crust that has tilted all the layers of rock near Cottonwood Wash to an almost vertical position. About four miles south of the turnoff to Grosvenor Arch, Cottonwood Wash (34) cuts through the sandstone layers of the Cockscomb and then parallels the road all the way to the Paria River. Hackberry Canyon (36) is the only other major canyon to cut through the Cockscomb and enter Cottonwood Wash. The section of the road that parallels Cottonwood Wash is particularly beautiful, and photographers are often seen along the road during the fall when the leaves of the cottonwood trees turn bright yellow.

Near the end of the road, Cottonwood Wash joins the Paria River, which cuts a deep narrow canyon through the Cockscomb known as "the Box" (38). Cottonwood Wash Road follows the Paria River for roughly five miles before heading southeast for an additional six miles through a desolate area of shale badlands, which are particularly slippery and challenging to drive through if the road is wet.

Kodachrome Basin State Park (31)

Located nine miles south of Cannonville on Cottonwood Wash Road, this easily accessible state park offers the best camping facilities in the area. Firewood and showers are available at the campground, and individual campsites have picnic tables and barbecue pits. The monument charges a minimal day-use fee and has reasonable overnight camping fees. This is a good place to set up a base camp to explore the numerous side canyons of the Paria River.

The monument was established to preserve the area's unique erosional forms and cliffs. A number of short trails wind through the strange, vividly colored formations of Entrada Sandstone, which is the same formation that forms the majestic spires of Capitol Reef's Cathedral Valley and the odd-shaped rock formations of Goblin Valley.

Sand pipes, an uncommon geologic feature, are found within the monument. They are up to sixty feet high and cylindrical in shape. These pipes consist of sand that is larger grained and more resistant than in the surrounding sandstone. As a result, the softer more-erodible sediments that surrounded the pipes have been removed, leaving what we see today.

One possible explanation for the formation of sand pipes is that they are the fossilized vents of ancient hot springs and geysers that were prevalent in the area ages ago.

Rock Springs Creek (32)

Overview
Rock Springs Creek is a fairly narrow canyon that cuts through the White Cliffs. This canyon is easily accessible from Cottonwood Wash Road and is a good entry/exit point for a backpacking trip along the Paria River. Some unusual petroglyphs are found at the junction of Rock Springs Creek and the Paria River.

Access
The turnoff to Rock Springs Creek is on the right side of Cottonwood Wash Road about a mile past the turn to Kodachrome Basin. Look for this unmarked road just before passing a BLM sign indicating the boundary of the Kanab Resource Area. An old corral is located on the left side of the road a half mile south of Cottonwood Wash Road. Continue driving until the road crosses Rock Springs Creek about two miles south of Cottonwood Wash Road. Shortly after crossing the creek, the road divides at another old corral. At this junction take a right after you pass over a cattle guard. Cross the stream twice more before

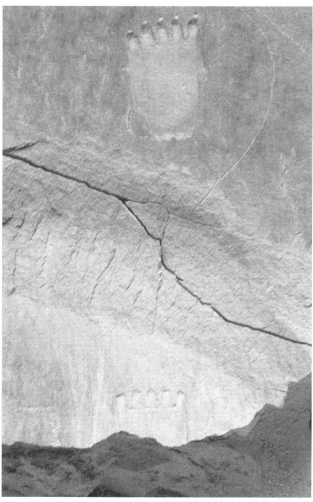

**Petroglyphs at the junction of
Rock Springs Creek and the Paria River**

Rock Springs Creek

parking; four-wheel-drive might be helpful in some sandy sections. Low-clearance vehicles should park where the stream first crosses the road (parking here only adds about three-quarters of a mile to the hike).

Difficulty

Hiking along Rock Springs Creek is easy, and the stream is small enough to jump across without getting your feet wet. It is about a seven-mile round-trip hike to the junction of Rock Springs Creek and the Paria River.

Maps

1:24,000 Slickrock Bench, Bull Valley Gorge
1:100,000 Smoky Mountain, Kanab

Elevation

5,700 feet to 5,500 feet

Water

Both the Paria River and Rock Springs Creek carry a lot of sediment.

Camping

Backpackers can find numerous camping sites along the Paria River. Car campers could use the established campground at Kodachrome State Park. Most of the small roads that take off from the road to Rock Springs Creek lead to sites suitable for car camping.

Route Description

Rock Springs Creek runs through a broad wash that is surrounded by the multicolored badlands of the Carmel Formation, a set of rock layers above the Navajo Sandstone of the White Cliffs. Ripple marks from the waves of an ancient sea are preserved on many of the flat rock surfaces. Giant ponderosa pine trees line the distant cliffs. Gambel oak and cottonwood trees grow along the wash, but the vegetation is not thick enough to be an obstruction.

The canyon changes dramatically about a mile after leaving the road. As Rock Springs Creek begins to cut into the Navajo Sandstone, it forms a deep-walled narrow canyon. The canyon becomes continuously deeper and narrower as it approaches the intersection with the Paria. At one point the canyon narrows to as little as ten feet. You may see tracks of deer and coyote scattered about the canyon floor.

Just before joining the Paria River, Rock Springs Creek makes a sharp bend to the north past an isolated rock pillar. Some unusual petroglyphs are located on this rock pillar and are found on the side of the rock facing the Paria River. The petroglyphs are about eye level and resemble bear tracks. A few much-older and less-distinct petroglyphs can be seen along this same panel.

The canyon of the Paria is 500 to 600 feet deep where Rock Spring Creek enters. Hiking any distance up or down the Paria requires wading across the knee-deep river. Rock Springs Creek makes an excellent entrance/exit for backpackers wishing to hike the Paria River (43). Deer Creek Canyon is about seven miles down the Paria River from its junction with Rock Springs Creek. Water can be obtained at some springs found on the west side of the Paria River about two miles away.

Round Valley Draw (33)

Overview
This is perhaps the deepest and most narrow slot canyon within the monument. A number of choke stones and dry-falls most be negotiated, making this a challenging hike.

Access
Drive fifteen miles southeast from Cannonville on Cottonwood Wash Road and take a left at the marked road leading to Rush Beds. This road is located just past Round Valley Draw (the wash), which is also indicated by a sign. South of Cottonwood Wash Road, the road to Rush Beds crosses Round Valley Draw after a mile and a half. You can either park where the road crosses Round Valley Draw or drive down Draw wash a short distance before parking. Rush Beds Road is rough in a few spots, and a high-clearance vehicle is recommended.

Difficulty
The first mile and a half of hiking through the narrows is quite difficult and involves climbing up and down dry-falls and over choke stones. Negotiating these obstacles requires good upper-body strength. People who do not have a lot of upper-body strength should bring along a hiking partner for help. Hiking the last mile and a half is much easier. It is three miles from the start of the narrows to the intersection of Round Valley Draw and Hackberry Canyon.

Maps
1:100,000 Smoky Mountain
1:24,000 Slickrock Bench

Elevation
6,000 fcct to 5,800 feet

Water
Bring your own.

Round Valley Draw

Camping

There are developed campgrounds at Kodachrome Basin State Park and Grosvenor Arch, and more primitive car camping at various pull-offs along Cottonwood Wash Road.

Route Description

The narrows begin a mile downstream where Round Valley Draw wash intersects Rush Beds Road. Most of this distance can be driven in a four-wheel-drive vehicle. The upper section of the canyon is quite broad, and the rolling hills and cliffs on either side of the wash are covered by juniper forests.

The slot canyon begins forming as soon as the creek bed intersects the Navajo Sandstone of the White Cliffs. It is best to enter into the narrows as soon as you start to cut into the sandstone, although this is a little difficult. Once in the narrows, the first half mile is easy hiking. The convoluted sandstone walls and intricate texturing, a result of cross-bedding in the sandstone, make the first half mile of the narrows very good for photography.

The deepest section of the narrows is encountered after a large rockfall three-quarters of a mile from the start of the narrows. Getting over this rockfall is the most serious obstacle in the canyon. The obstacle is not a problem if you have a climbing partner or if you have good upper-body strength. The canyon widens a quarter of a mile down from this rockfall, and only one more small set of narrows is present farther down the canyon.

Even at its widest, Round Valley Draw is a very deep and narrow canyon. The absence of water in the canyon results in very little vegetation in the stream bottom. The steep canyon walls are dotted with juniper, pinyon pine, and even a few ponderosa pine trees.

Cottonwood Wash Narrows (34)

Overview

This short hike goes through some fantastic narrows and is easily accessible from Cottonwood Wash Road. The small section of narrows cuts dramatically through the folded sandstone layers of the Cockscomb.

Access

From the Grosvenor Arch turnoff, drive south another four miles on Cottonwood Wash Road, which makes a steep descent before crossing a small wash at the bottom of the hill. This is the steepest grade along the entire length of Cottonwood Wash Road, so it is quite distinctive. Park near the wash at the bottom of the hill where a small rock pillar can be seen near the road.

If heading north from Highway 89 on Cottonwood Wash Road, drive about five and a half miles past the marked turnoff for Pack Springs to the base of the steep hill where the parking area is.

Difficulty

This very easy hike is just a little over two miles round-trip.

Maps

1:100,000 Smoky Mountain
1:24,000 Butler Valley

Elevation

6,000 feet

Water

Bring your own.

Camping

There are established campgrounds at Kodachrome Basin State Park and Grosvenor Arch. More primitive car camping can be found at pullouts along Cottonwood Wash Road.

Route Description

Upon entering the canyon it is possible to go either upstream or downstream. A short hike upstream about a quarter of a mile goes through the best section of narrows in Cottonwood Wash. After exploring the narrows upstream, turn around and follow the canyon downstream to where it intersects the road after one and a quarter miles.

The short hike down the canyon is spectacular as the canyon cuts through the folded layers of the Cockscomb. The canyon walls remain deep and colorful, and a few little side canyons make some exploration possible. A wide variety of plants are found within the canyon, including Mormon tea, buffaloberry, phlox, paintbrush, prickly pear, single-leaf ash, and juniper trees.

The canyon walls quickly give way as the wash nears the road, just below the large power lines that can be seen running north-south. Walk up the road about three-quarters of a mile to get back to the parking area.

The Cockscomb Cross-Country Route/Castle Rock (35)

Overview
This hike follows a seldom-used route to an area of cliffs, pinnacles, rock towers, sandstone fins, and narrows. Excellent views of Castle Rock, a large sandstone monolith that towers above the rest of the Cockscomb, can be seen along this route. Some scrambling and route finding along the washes and ridges of the Cockscomb make this a moderately challenging day hike that is very similar to hiking in Capitol Reef along the top of the Waterpocket Fold.

Access
The location of this trailhead is best described in relation to Hackberry Canyon Trailhead (36). Drive north of the pullout for the Hackberry Canyon Trail, cross over a small wash, and go past a large rock outcrop on the right side of the road. After passing the rock outcrop, watch for jeep trails taking off on the left side of the road. Continue driving past the first jeep trail, and take a left at the second one (both of these side roads are within a mile of the rock outcrop and wash). Park along this second jeep trail a few hundred yards after it ends near Cottonwood Wash.

Difficulty
Some sections of the route are a little steep, particularly the first quarter of a mile. Route finding is necessary as no established trail exists. The length of the described route is about three miles round-trip. Longer hikes are possible for those wanting to explore the area.

Maps
1:24,000 Calico Peak
1:100,000 Smoky Mountain

Elevation
4,900 feet to 5,500 feet

Water
Bring your own.

Camping
Backpackers can find a number of places to set up camp along the described route. A good site for car camping is found at the trailhead parking area.

Route Description
From the parking area, look west toward the ridge of the Cockscomb. A small saddle on the ridge marks the mouth of a little canyon. Dark water stains on the white Navajo Sandstone just below the saddle also mark the mouth of this canyon. It is a steep climb for a third of a mile to the mouth of the canyon. From the top of the climb, be sure to follow the westward-running drainage and not the more-northerly fork that parallels the Cockscomb.

Heading west, the small canyon is filled with ponderosa pine trees, single-leaf ash trees, oak trees, and bitterbrush. The walking is easy among the slickrock-stained waterways, plunge pools, and sandy wash bottom.

The canyon forks after a half mile. Follow the right fork and continue another three-quarters of a mile to the top of a ridge. The drainage leading to the ridge can be difficult to follow as it divides many times, but all that is important is to continue north. The ridge offers great views of Castle Rock and the maze of sandstone fins and pinnacles that surround it.

Continue north and descend off the ridge into an east-west-running canyon. Follow this canyon upstream a half mile to some sandstone fins that would look quite at home in Arches National Park. This entire area is an intriguing place for cross-country exploring. The edge of the giant cliffs overlooking Hackberry Canyon is only a few miles to the west. When leaving the area, keep in mind that many of the canyons that head east back toward Cottonwood Wash Road end in dry-falls that cannot be descended.

Hackberry Canyon

Hackberry Canyon (upper & lower) (36)

Overview
This deep and narrow canyon cuts through the sandstone cliffs of the Cockscomb and makes either a good day hike or a backpacking trip. A small stream runs through the very colorful and dramatic sandstone walls of the canyon. This canyon is easily accessed from Cottonwood Wash Road.

Access
Upper Hackberry Canyon
Drive twelve miles south of Cannonville on Cottonwood Wash Road. The road to Hackberry Canyon takes off to the right just after passing the entrance sign to the monument. A high-clearance vehicle may be helpful for driving along the mile-and-a-half-long side road that leads to the canyon. Park where a small fence crosses the wash.

Lower Hackberry Canyon
Located thirty-four miles south of Cannonville on Cottonwood Wash Road or twelve miles north of Highway 89, Hackberry Canyon is one of the few large canyons to cut through the Cockscomb. The mouth of this canyon is easily seen from the road. The trailhead is not marked by a sign, but a pullout is located along Cottonwood Wash Road for trailhead parking.

Difficulty
The hiking is generally easy, and the stream is small enough that crossings are not a problem. Hiking is more difficult during the winter months as the small wash becomes filled with ice. It is five miles one way to Sam Pollack Arch, and hiking all the way through the canyon is an eighteen-mile trip that requires a car shuttle. From the upper end it is a hike of two miles one way to the junction with Round Valley Draw.

Maps
1:100,000 Smoky Mountain
1:24,000 Calico Peak, Slickrock Bench
Elevation
Top: 6,000 feet

Upper Hackberry

Water

A small creek runs through most of the canyon. The upper part of the canyon above the junction with Round Valley Draw is dry.

Camping

Backpackers can find good campsites in Hackberry Canyon, and good locations for car camping are available at pullouts along Cottonwood Wash Road.

Route Description

Upper Hackberry Canyon

The canyon starts out as a broad wash that quickly deepens and narrows. Starting about a half mile below the fence, Hackberry Canyon is closed to vehicles. The upper sections of the canyon are quite narrow, and giant ponderosa pine trees grow profusely.

I tried getting into the upper section of the canyon from Upper Slickrock Bench, but this proved impossible due to the canyon's steep cliffs. An interesting possibility for a day hike if a car shuttle is possible is to hike down Hackberry Canyon and out Round Valley Draw (33).

Lower Hackberry Canyon

From Cottonwood Wash Road, Hackberry Canyon heads west through the sandstone cliffs of the Cockscomb. Hackberry Canyon is quite narrow for the first two miles as it cuts through the Navajo Sandstone portion of the Cockscomb.

The Navajo Sandstone of Hackberry Canyon is richly painted in orange and red hues that are mixed with the brown-and-black colors of desert varnish. Of all the canyons in the monument, the sandstone walls of Hackberry Canyon display the most brilliant mix of colors. The bright-green leaves of the cottonwood trees are beautifully offset against the darker canyon walls.

The canyon begins cutting into the less-resistant deep-red sandstones of the Kayenta and Wingate Formations a mile and a half from the road, then begins to slowly widen.

Sam Pollack Arch is a good destination found in a side canyon to the left of Hackberry Canyon, four miles up from the trailhead.

THE COCKSCOMB

The Cockscomb is known to geologists as the East Kaibab Monocline. Rocks folded in a manner similar to those of the Cockscomb are classified as monoclines. The East Kaibab Monocline is almost a hundred miles long.

Folds form in response to compressive forces active in the earth's crust. These compressive forces often result from large-scale plate movements.

The Waterpocket Fold in Capitol Reef is perhaps the most well-known monocline. The Cockscomb is very similar in structure to the Waterpocket Fold.

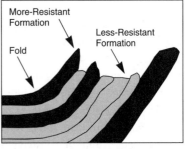

To the visitor, the fold appears as a series of serrated ridges; a ridge of this type is often referred to as a hogback. The ridges form as a result of differential erosion. The more-resistant rock layers stand out as ridges and the less-resistant form the intervening low areas. The rocks of the Cockscomb have been so steeply tilted that it is easy to see the actual tilt of the various rock layers.

Begin looking for this side canyon just after you pass the remains of an old cabin, located on the left side of the creek. Hike a mile and a half up this side canyon to the arch, which is easy to spot. Its exact location is shown on topographic maps of the area.

Hackberry Canyon continues another fourteen miles to where it comes out near the upper stretches of Cottonwood Wash Road.

The Cockscomb Overlook (37)

Overview

The double ridge of the Cockscomb results from a giant fold in the sedimentary rock layers in the region. One of the best places to get a view of this fold is from the road that goes up and over the Cockscomb to Brigham Plains. A short hike to the top of the Cockscomb offers great views of the folded layers of the Cockscomb and the cliffs of the Grand Staircase.

Access

The road that goes over the Cockscomb takes off from the left (east) side of Cottonwood Wash Road, thirty-seven miles southwest of Cannonville (thirteen miles north of Highway 89). Drive south one-fifth of a mile past the pull-off for Hackberry Canyon Trail (36), and take a left on the unmarked road that goes up and over the Cockscomb. The road is quite steep and is a little rough near the top. Park where the road reaches the top of the Cockscomb, a mile east from Cottonwood Wash Road.

Difficulty

The round-trip hike is one and a half miles long and is quite steep. There is no established trail, but the route is easy to pick out. To get a good view of the Cockscomb, drive about halfway up the side road mentioned in the access section.

Maps

1:100,000 Smoky Mountain
1:24,000 Five-Mile Valley/Calico Peak

Elevation

5,300 feet to 5,700 feet

Water

None

Camping

Pullouts along Cottonwood Wash Road provide good places for car camping.

Route Description

Extending all the way from Highway 12 to the Arizona border, the Cockscomb is a fold very similar in form to the Waterpocket Fold in Capitol Reef. It is possible to actually see the tilting of the various sedimentary layers. The layers that form prominent ridges are more resistant to erosion. The least-resistant sedimentary layers do not stand out at all and form the small valley of Cottonwood Wash.

The best views of the folded layers of the Cockscomb and cliffs of the Grand Staircase are from the very top of the knife-edged ridge of the Cockscomb. The top of the Cockscomb is three-quarters of a mile from the car park and, since it is easily visible, picking a route is not difficult.

The Cockscomb exposes all of the rock formations present in the monument. The tilting of the layers allows a large number of rock formations to be exposed across a relatively short distance

The mineral barite fills in numerous fractures in the sandstone that makes up the tall ridge of the Cockscomb. Barite is the same mineral that forms the desert roses commonly seen in rock shops.

The Box Section of the Paria/Shurtz Gorge (38)

Overview

Where the Paria River cuts through the Cockscomb, it enters a deep narrow gorge known as "the Box." The Box section of the Paria River is about 900 feet deep and a mile in length. This short hike is easily reached from either the Old Paria Town Site (42) or from Cottonwood Wash Road.

Access from Old Paria

From the ghost town of Old Paria (42), park and walk down the Paria River a little less than a mile to the Box.

Access from Cottonwood Wash Road

Drive two and a half miles south of Hackberry Canyon Trailhead. Watch for the confluence of the Paria River and Cottonwood Wash. Park as soon as the Paria River appears on the right and hike up the river. A small road branches from Cottonwood Wash Road on the right and heads a short distance toward the Paria River.

Difficulty

Hiking is easy along the flat banks of the Paria River. To hike all the way through the Box requires wading the knee-deep Paria River. This hike is roughly two and a half miles round-trip.

Maps

1:100,000 Smoky Mountain
1:24,000 Five-Mile Valley

Elevation
4,700 feet

Water
The water in the Paria River carries a lot of sediment.

Camping
There is good car camping at pullouts along Cottonwood Wash Road and near the town site of Old Paria (42).

Route Description (described from the Old Paria Town Site)
To reach the Box, hike a mile down the Paria River from the Old Paria Town Site. This is easy hiking, but the river must be crossed a few times. Before entering the Box, the Paria River runs across a wide plain, and the multicolored hills and buttes of the Chinle Formation can be seen in the distance. You will pass an old ranch house on the east bank of the Paria River before entering the Box.

The Box cuts through the sedimentary layers of the Cockscomb. Most of the sedimentary rocks in the monument lie in a horizontal position, but the rocks of the Cockscomb have been tilted so that they lie in an almost vertical position. As a result, the short hike through the Box crosses many sedimentary layers.

As the Paria River begins to carve through the tilted layers of the Cockscomb, it becomes even narrower. Some caves are present in the Navajo Sandstone along the west bank when the Box reaches its narrowest point. The Paria River Canyon quickly widens as it approaches the confluence with Cottonwood Wash. Once the Paria begins to widen, Cottonwood Wash Road can be reached by heading due east.

HIGHWAY 89: ROUTE DESCRIPTION

Highway 89 traverses the southern boundary of the monument between the towns of Kanab and Big Water. The highway parallels the base of the Vermilion Cliffs most of the way through the monument. It was built in the late 1950s to connect Glen Canyon Dam with the more populous areas of Utah.

Kanab is one of the larger towns adjacent to the monument's boundaries, and it is easy to find a hotel or grocery store in this city. Heading east on Highway 89 from Kanab, the Skutumpah/Johnson Canyon Road takes off to the left eight miles east of Kanab. This forty-six-mile road connects Highway 89 to Highway 12 and provides access to a number of tributaries of the Paria River (*see* Skutumpah Road on page 151).

Continuing east on Highway 89 along the base of the Vermilion Cliffs, Nipple Ranch Road (*see* Nipple Ranch Road on page 144) takes off to the left precisely at milepost thirty-seven. This graded dirt road located twenty miles east of Kanab provides access to Mollies Nipple (47), Mollies Lake, Park Wash, and Deer Springs Canyon (46).

The road to the ghost town of Old Paria (42) and the Old Paria Movie Set (41), takes off to the left of Highway 89 between mileposts thirty and thirty-one, twenty-seven miles east of Kanab (*see* Movie Set Road on page 136). This road is also used by hikers wanting access to the Paria River (43).

Driving east on Highway 89 from Movie Set Road, the Cockscomb is seen straight ahead as a long, north-south-trending ridge. The road crosses the double-ridged spine of the Cockscomb and descends into the Paria River Valley. Before crossing over the second ridge of the Cockscomb, House Rock Valley Road takes off to the right and gives access to Kaibab and Buckskin Gulches. The tilted-rock layers of the Cockscomb are not displayed as well along Highway 89 in comparison to Cottonwood Wash Road.

Just after crossing the Paria River, White House Road takes off on the right and travels two and a half miles to a small campground and the very popular Lower Paria River Trailhead. This trail, located in the Paria Canyon/Vermilion Cliffs Wilderness Area, is not described in this guide, but information is obtainable at a ranger station located at the junction of Highway 89 and White House Road.

Three miles after Highway 89 crosses the Paria River, Cottonwood Wash Road takes off to the left. Cottonwood Wash Road, connecting Highway 89 to Highway 12, is one of the scenic drives in the monument (*see* Cottonwood Wash Road on page 114).

Continuing on Highway 89 past the turnoff to Cottonwood Wash Road, the highway leaves the boundaries of the monument. Smoky Mountain Road connects with Highway 89 at the town of Big Water (*see* Smoky Mountain Road on page 78). No services are available in Big Water, but all services can be found in Page, Arizona, fifteen miles east of Big Water. The town of Greene is only six miles east of Big Water and has a gas station that is open year-round.

Kaibab Gulch (40)

This 800-foot-deep gorge provides a good look at some of the monument's oldest rocks. The mouth of Kaibab Gulch is located a short distance from the popular Buckskin Gulch Trailhead and is often overlooked by hikers.

The House Rock Valley Road takes off from U.S. 89 and heads south about thirty-five miles east of Kanab. Drive south on this road about four miles and the gulch will be on the west side of the road just before the Buckskin Gulch area.

Of all the hikes in this book, Kaibab Gulch is at the lowest elevation, and it is the only canyon mentioned so far whose walls are made of limestone. The Kaibab Limestone that forms the canyon was named after Kaibab Gulch. Rock formations are often named after places where they are well exposed.

The Kaibab Limestone was deposited in an ancient ocean during the Permian period (270 million years ago). Marine fossils can be seen within this limestone. The distance between the sandstone narrows of Buckskin Gulch and the limestone walls of Kaibab Gulch is small, but the canyons are markedly different.

White House Road/Campground (39)

This campground is located on White House Road two and a half miles south of the junction with Highway 89. Turn right at the ranger station near where Highway 89 crosses the Paria River. This is a small, primitive campground with picnic tables, fire pits, and restrooms and is generally crowded due to its proximity to the Paria Canyon Narrows Trailhead.

Old Movie Set

MOVIE SET ROAD: ROUTE DESCRIPTION

Movie Set Road heads north from Highway 89 between mileposts thirty and thirty-one, twenty-seven miles east of Kanab. The turnoff along Highway 89 is well marked, and this is a well-graded road, passable to all types of vehicles.

The road offers exceptional views of the Vermilion Cliffs and the Badlands, which are made up of the multicolored Chinle Formation. The Old Movie Set is five miles north of Highway 89, and the ghost town of Old Paria and the Paria River are seven miles north of Highway 89. The last two miles of the road are fairly rough, but in dry weather even a passenger car should be able to make it.

Old Paria Movie Set (41)

Located five miles north of Highway 89 on Movie Set Road, the Old Paria Movie Set consists of a collection of old buildings that were built specifically as a movie set. Their exteriors were decorated when movies were being filmed, but indoor scenes were filmed on sets in Hollywood. The buildings retain the look of an old western town, and it is fun to wander around and take pictures.

The multicolored hills of the Chinle Formation make an excellent backdrop to the movie set. It is little wonder that this beautiful area attracted Hollywood's attention. The set was originally made for the filming of the movie *Sergeants Three* but was later used for numerous other films.

The BLM has set up a picnic area adjacent to the Old Paria Movie Set. It is seldom crowded, and no fees are charged. Barbecue pits can be found at the picnic site, but wood is hard to find in the vicinity.

Old Paria Town (42)

To reach the ghost town of Old Paria, continue driving on Movie Set Road past the Old Movie Set. The road becomes rough but is passable in good weather. The Old Paria cemetery is located a half mile up the road from the movie set. The tombstones are old and weathered. A monument has been erected to identify and commemorate the people buried here.

The road can be driven almost all the way to the Paria River. A number of old ranch houses are located on the opposite bank, so getting to these houses requires wading across the knee-deep Paria River.

Old Paria was settled in the early 1870s by Mormon pioneers. Cattle grazed in the valley and crops grew along the river. A number of floods in the 1880s made agriculture difficult, and the town was abandoned. The remains of a few old ranches can also be found farther up the Paria River.

Hiking the Paria River (43)

Overview

The thirty-mile stretch of the Paria River between Cannonville and Highway 89 offers one of the monument's best backpacking trips. It passes through some of the most isolated and remote country in the lower forty-eight states and is often overlooked by hikers who are attracted to the more popular lower section of the Paria River between Highway 89 and the Colorado River (Lee's Ferry).

Paria River

The Paria River cuts through both the Vermilion and the White Cliffs of the Grand Staircase. A number of side canyons can be explored leading to arches, petroglyphs, and waterfalls. The petroglyphs found along the Paria display a wide variety of styles and ages.

Access
This route begins near the Old Paria Movie Set (41). Drive a mile and a half past the movie set and park near the Paria River. No established trail or trailhead exists for this hike.

On the northern end of the monument, the Paria River is accessed via Rock Springs Creek (32). A complete one-way trip through the canyon requires a long car shuttle between Movie Set Road and the northwest end of Cottonwood Wash Road. A backpacking trip or day hike up or down the river from either of the two starting points can be just as rewarding.

Difficulty
Hiking up the Paria River requires numerous stream crossings so it is best to wear wading shoes. The most interesting sections of the Paria River are above the junction with Kitchen Creek, which is four miles upstream from the trailhead. To locate specific side canyons, use a good map and count off the various side canyons and meanders as you travel upstream.

Maps (from south to north)
1:100,000 Smoky Mountain, Kanab
1:24,000 Five-mile Valley, Calico Peak, Deer Range Point, Bull Valley Gorge

Elevation
4,800 feet

Water
The water of the Paria River is full of fine sediment and is not of very good drinking quality. Water coming in from sources such as Kitchen Canyon, Hogeye, Oak, and Deer Creeks is of better quality but should be treated. Seeps and springs in the area are a good water source. One spring is located just before the mouth of Hogeye, and another, Crack Spring, is about a mile past Deer Creek Canyon.

Camping

Backpackers can find numerous good camping spots along the Paria River. The best camping locations are at the mouths of Kitchen Creek, Hogeye Creek, and Deer Creek because of the presence of clear-running water. Car camping is possible at the trailhead.

Route Description

Paria River Canyon is quite wide near the trailhead as it travels through the multicolored badlands of the Chinle Formation. The canyon begins to narrow when it cuts into the Vermilion Cliffs, about two and a half miles upstream from the trailhead.

An old road exists on the west bank of the Paria River, three-quarters of a mile upstream from the trailhead. Walking along this road is a lot easier than trying to follow the meandering course of the river. To locate the road, head west away from the Paria River at the drainage that comes down between Calico Peak and No Mans Mesa. The road previously ran between the town of Old Paria and some ranches upstream. Remains of one of the ranch houses are found along the road.

Paria River Canyon gradually narrows and deepens as it begins to cut into the Vermilion Cliffs. The canyon of the Paria is quite impressive by the time Kitchen Canyon (44) is reached. This canyon is easily recognized because it is the only side canyon, so far, to have flowing water. Its mouth is a good spot to camp, and a hike up the canyon makes a good side trip.

Petroglyphs can be found at the mouth of Kitchen Canyon. They are located at the base of the canyon walls on the north side of the junction between the canyon and the Paria River. The rock art consists of human figures and abstract concentric circles. The petroglyphs are very faded and probably quite old.

Upstream from the junction with Kitchen Canyon, the canyon of the Paria begins to meander. Shortcuts can be made across the meanders by following ATV tracks. The tracks are made by local ranchers who are allowed to use them for herding cattle.

Hogeye Canyon takes off to the right a mile upstream from the junction with Kitchen Canyon. Good drinking water can be obtained from springs located in an alcove that sits at a large bend in the river just before the mouth of Hogeye. Look for cottonwood trees and a trickle of water coming down to the left side of the Paria River.

Upstream from Hogeye, the Paria River Canyon continues to narrow and deepen. Snake Creek enters on the right, four miles upstream from Hogeye Canyon. Snake Creek is easily missed as it has a narrow opening that is obscured by brush. Oak Creek enters from the left, another mile and a half past Snake Creek. Oak Canyon has an intermittent water flow.

A mile past Oak Canyon, Deer Creek Canyon enters the Paria on the left. The White Cliffs come into view just before the junction with Deer Creek Canyon. There are petroglyphs at the Junction of Deer Creek and the Paria, located on the north side of the mouth of Deer Creek and facing the Paria River. Look carefully, as they are scattered along the canyon walls for about sixty feet, and most of them are quite faint. The rock art depicts abstract figures, including a double circle with spokes radiating outward like a wagon wheel, and some decorated human figures. This rock art looks much older and is a different style than the petroglyphs up Deer Creek Canyon.

Deer Creek Canyon is one of the best side canyons of the Paria to explore. Some interesting pictographs and petroglyphs are found a third of a mile up the canyon, located in an alcove on the north side of the canyon. These pictographs are painted in green, yellow, and red, and consist of humanlike figures and handprints. The yellow and green colors are quite unusual for the monument. Two miles upstream from Deer Creek, waterfalls block further progress up the canyon. Good camping can be found in the secluded area near the falls.

Up the Paria from Deer Creek Canyon the canyon walls are rimmed with Navajo Sandstone. Large alcoves have formed into the Navajo Sandstone high above the canyon floor. Clear-flowing water can be obtained from Crack Spring, a mile and a half up the canyon from Deer Creek.

The rest of the trip up the Paria is described under Rock Springs Creek (32). An alternative to exiting the Paria via Rock Springs

Creek is to exit the canyon via Willis Creek (50). Exiting via Bull Valley Gorge would be a poor choice because carrying packs through this narrow canyon would be difficult.

Kitchen and Starlight Canyons (side trip from Paria River) (44)

Overview

Kitchen and Starlight Canyons are good destinations reached by a long day hike or a backpacking trip. Kitchen Falls cascades over a sandstone overhang into a large pool. Some unusual narrows and springs are found up Starlight Canyon. The whole area is a desert oasis.

Access

Kitchen Canyon enters the Paria from the left and is reached by hiking four miles up the Paria River from the Old Paria Town Site. Kitchen Canyon is the only side canyon of the Paria that has any running water in this four-mile stretch. Starlight Canyon is a side canyon of Kitchen Canyon.

Another possible access route runs from Nipple Ranch Road (*see* Nipple Ranch Road on page 144). However, the route into the canyon from Nipple Lake crosses private property. It might be possible to enter Starlight Canyon from the base of Mollies Nipple (47).

Difficulty

The four-mile hike up the Paria River is fairly easy. Hikes up the Paria River and Kitchen and Starlight Canyons require some wading. It's two miles up Kitchen Canyon to Kitchen Falls and a mile up Starlight Canyon to the narrows.

Maps

1:100,000 Kanab, Smoky Mountain
1:24,000 Deer Range Point, Calico Peak

Elevation

5,500 to 6,000 feet

Water

Some good springs are found in the narrows of Starlight Canyon; make sure to treat the water from Kitchen Canyon.

Camping

Backpackers can camp at the junction of Kitchen Canyon and the Paria River.

Kitchen Falls

Route Description

As you cut through the Wingate Sandstone of the Vermilion Cliffs, you will notice that the walls of Kitchen Canyon are deep red. Giant cottonwood trees with masses of green leaves provide a pleasing contrast to the red canyon walls. The easiest walking is right in the creek bed because of steep banks and thick vegetation on either side of the creek.

Kitchen Falls is located two miles up the canyon from the Paria River. These beautiful waters cascade over a sandstone overhang into a large pool and are an excellent destination on a hot summer day. It is possible to continue up the canyon by scrambling up the steep slope on the right side of the falls. Upstream there are some ruins of old ranch houses, and Nipple Lake is about three miles past the falls.

Starlight Canyon, a side canyon of Kitchen Canyon, heads to the left just before Kitchen Falls. The water in Starlight Canyon is noticeably colder than the water in Kitchen Canyon. The water is emitted from numerous seeps present between the mouth of the canyon and a short section of narrows farther upstream. These seeps occur near the canyon bottom along the contact between the Chinle Formation and Wingate Sandstone, providing places for water-loving plant communities to grow.

A short section of narrows is found a mile up Starlight Canyon. The narrows of the canyon are cut into the Kayenta Formation. The formation of narrows within the Kayenta is unusual because of the Kayenta's multilayered character. One seep in the narrows practically shoots out water and is a good place to fill a canteen. The narrows end in a small slide/dry-fall that is easy to climb. Not much water exists in the canyon above the narrows. From the top of Starlight Canyon it is possible to climb all the way to the top of Mollies Nipple, which would be a very long day hike.

Nipple Ranch Road: Route Description

Nipple Ranch Road offers excellent views of the White and Vermilion Cliffs as well as Mollies Nipple and Nipple Lake. Rock art and Indian ruins are found near the road and make for good side trips. Nipple Ranch Road heads north from Highway 89 at milepost thirty-seven, twenty miles east of Kanab. It is a well-graded road all the way to the Mollies Nipple turnoff.

No Mans Mesa

This remote plateau, ringed by cliffs 800 feet high, is located between Johnson Canyon and Nipple Ranch Road. Access to the base of the mesa is very difficult, and very few people, if any, ever visit the top. Due to its inaccessibility, No Mans Mesa has never been exploited by man for traditional uses such as ranching or logging. Good views of the mesa can be seen from the top of Deer Springs Canyon.

The result of this isolation is that plant communities have been little altered. Scientists can study these communities to understand what healthy ecosystems look like, which allows us to better manage and restore damaged plant areas.

King Mine, a historic mining site, can be found by driving three miles north on Nipple Ranch Road. Look for a three-way intersection and then continue another eighth of a mile before taking a right on a small side road. A half mile past the side road leading to the mine, several old mining structures can be see from Nipple Ranch Road.

This road approaches the Vermilion Cliffs three miles past the turnoff to King Mine. As the road gets closer to the cliffs it begins to parallel Park Wash. Park Wash is a scenic canyon that cuts through the Vermilion Cliffs. Deer Springs Canyon (46), an interesting side trip, takes off to the left just before the road enters the actual canyon of Park Wash.

Some pictographs can be seen in Park Wash on the right side of Nipple Ranch Road. They are located at the mouth of a small canyon that enters Park Wash, a mile past Box Elder Canyon, or three and a half miles past where the fence crosses the road. Drive slowly and examine all the rock outcrops that are visible from the road. The pictographs are quite faded, but the humanlike figure is interesting because of its unusual proportions. Additional pictographs can be found upstream on the left side of Park Wash.

At the first marked junction, ten miles north of Highway 89, Nipple Ranch Road continues to the right, and a high-clearance, four-wheel-drive road continues up Park Wash to the left. Nipple Ranch Road heads up a small side canyon of Park Wash toward the top of the Vermilion Cliffs. The marked road to Mollies Nipple (47) takes off to the right a mile before Nipple Ranch Road reaches a small pass at the top of the Vermilion cliffs.

Views of the White Cliffs, Mollies Nipple, and the side canyons of the Paria are excellent from the top of the small pass on the Nipple Ranch Road. Toward Nipple Ranch the road makes a steep decline and then becomes quite sandy in the vicinity of Nipple Lake, which is an unusual feature in this desert landscape. Kitchen Creek drains out of Nipple Lake and, following Kitchen Creek to the east, would make a good route into Kitchen Canyon (44). However, the area around Nipple Lake is currently private property. Nipple Ranch Road continues another mile or so over rough terrain to Starlight Ridge.

King Mine (45)

To reach this historic mining site, drive three miles north on Nipple Ranch Road. Look for a three-way intersection on the right side of the road. From this intersection drive another half mile on Nipple Ranch Road and turn at the first side road on the right. If you miss this road, you will pass some mining structures adjacent to Nipple Ranch Road. Drive up the side road less than a mile to the old mining site.

Remains of the mine, tailings piles, and an old dam that was used to catch water can be seen at the mining site. Miners began looking for magnesium at this site in the early 1940s, and at one point more than twenty people worked at the mine. However, it proved difficult to separate the magnesium ores from the clays of the Chinle Formation, and the mine was completely abandoned by the late 1950s. Magnesium ore is heavy, dark-green material, and some nice specimens can be found (however, collecting is illegal).

Additional mining structures can be seen along Nipple Ranch Road. The miners even tried to dam Park Wash adjacent to Nipple Ranch Road to secure water for the mining operation.

Deer Springs Canyon (46)

Deer Springs Canyon is a scenic canyon that cuts through the Vermilion Cliffs. Some interesting pictographs are located in its upper reaches.

To get to Deer Springs Canyon, follow Nipple Ranch Road for five miles to where a fence crosses the road, and then continue about another mile to where the road to Deer Springs Canyon takes off on the left. This road immediately crosses Park Wash before heading up Deer Springs Canyon. It is a very poor road and should only be driven by people who enjoy the challenges offered by four-wheel-drive roads. This would also be a nice canyon to hike.

Pictographs at Deer Springs Canyon

Two miles farther up Deer Springs Canyon you will pass a fence. Drive or walk another one and a half miles past the fence to find the pictographs. Once the White Cliffs come into view, start looking for the pictographs on the left side of the canyon. The pictographs are in an alcove that is difficult to see from the wash, so it is necessary to look for them on foot. The pictographs are about a half mile down Deer Springs Canyon from Wild Cat Springs.

The pictographs are painted in white and black and are well preserved. They consist mostly of abstract shapes and figures such as circles and intricate triangular patterns.

Past the pictographs, Deer Springs Canyon opens up at the base of the White Cliffs in an area called Nephi's Pasture. The White Cliffs are divided into a series of large plateaus that are almost 1,000 feet tall. No Mans Mesa, which can be seen to the northeast, preserves a relict vegetation that is unaltered by man (*see* No Mans Mesa on page 145). The area at the base of the White Cliffs is open to exploration. Two alternate routes can be taken to get back to a main road: Little Fin Wash to Highway 89 or Johnson Lakes Canyon to Johnson Canyon Road. It is necessary to bring along a good topographic map when exploring this area. Expect rough driving conditions throughout.

Mollies Nipple (47)

Overview

At 7,271 feet, Mollies Nipple is one of the monument's highest points. The distinctive cone-like shape of Mollies Nipple makes it a good landmark, easily seen from many locations. Mollies Nipple is composed of Navajo Sandstone and is an erosional remnant of the White Cliffs.

Access

To reach Mollies Nipple, drive ten miles on Nipple Ranch Road and take a right at the marked junction that indicates Mollies Nipple is five miles. Continue another mile on this road before taking another right onto a smaller side road that heads east for another four miles to the base of Mollies Nipple. This is a high-clearance, four-wheel-drive road only and is very sandy. The sandy spots are much more easily negotiated after a light rain.

Mollies Nipple

Difficulty

The hike to the top of Mollies Nipple is a short but very steep hike up talus slopes. Of all the hikes in the book this is the steepest. Walking around the base of Mollies Nipple also offers very good views.

Map

1:24,000 Deer Range Point

Elevation

6,400 feet to 7,271 feet

Water

None

Camping

There is good car camping near the base of Mollies Nipple.

Route Description

Follow the road to the base of Mollies Nipple and park where the road forks to the left. The left fork of the road is in a Wilderness Study Area and vehicles are not allowed. Follow this small jeep trail on foot to the base of Mollies Nipple. The steep talus slopes of Mollies Nipple look intimidating at first but an easy route exists.

The easiest route appears to be on the west face of Mollies Nipple, and while you are climbing, you will have a fantastic view of the Grand Staircase and the Paria River drainage. From the top of Mollies Nipple the size of the monument and its remoteness can be easily appreciated.

Mollies Nipple is an erosional remnant of the White Cliffs. The dark-colored rock that caps Mollies Nipple and litters the slopes is the Carmel Formation. Perhaps this resistant rock protected Mollies Nipple from the effects of erosion.

West Swag (48)

This is about a twenty-minute walk to some seldom-visited ruins. The ruins are actually located in a wash just between the south and west swag. To reach the ruins follow Nipple Ranch Road past the turnoff to Mollies Nipple. The road reaches a high point at a small pass atop the Vermilion Cliffs before beginning a downgrade. As the road starts heading downhill, keep an eye on the cliffs that drop off on the right side of the road. When possible, scale down the cliffs and follow the cliff line south to an alcove that houses Indian ruins that are circular and made of bricks cemented together by clay. Some minor petroglyphs can be seen along the cliff walls near the ruins.

The Monkey House (49)

Built in 1896, the Monkey House is one of the most famous ranch sites in the monument. The builder, Dick Woolsey, his wife, and a large monkey lived there for over fifteen years. When visitors came, the monkey, which had its own house atop a pole, would chatter noisily. The Monkey House is built into a rock wall on the right side of the canyon.

To reach the Monkey House, follow Nipple Ranch Road fifteen miles to Nipple Ranch. Take a right off Nipple Ranch Road at a very sandy intersection near the base of the White Cliffs. This intersection

The Monkey House

is easily recognized because the sand here is very deep. Drive less than a mile and take a left just before reaching the locked gate to Nipple Ranch. The road to the left goes a few hundred feet before it turns left again and follows the Nipple Ranch fence line. The road ends at the end of the fence line after about a quarter of a mile. Park at the end of the road and follow the fence line to the east on foot for about a mile and a half to the Monkey House. The route goes right past Nipple Lake, but the lake is on private property.

SKUTUMPAH ROAD/JOHNSON CANYON: ROUTE DESCRIPTION

The Skutumpah/Johnson Canyon road runs north-south through the monument, connecting Highway 12 with Highway 89. To reach the road, drive four miles south of Cannonville on Cottonwood Wash

Road and take a right at the marked junction. Most of the road is unpaved except for the fifteen-mile section through Johnson Canyon, near Highway 89. The dirt and gravel sections of the road are well maintained, but the roadway can become quite slick in places during bad weather. The road is passable most of the year by most vehicles.

Skutumpah Road provides access to many of the tributaries of the Paria River, including the scenic and narrow slot canyon of Bull Valley Gorge. The northern portion of the road offers good views of the White and Pink Cliffs, and the southern part of the road cuts through the Vermilion Cliffs.

South of Cottonwood Wash Road the first twelve miles of Skutumpah Road are winding and slow going, as the road crosses numerous small washes and ridges. Of these small washes, only Sheep Creek and Willis Creek have water, since these small streams drain off the high plateau of Bryce Canyon. Sheep Creek is crossed about four miles south of Cottonwood Wash Road, and Willis Creek is about six miles south of the road.

Bull Valley Gorge, located nine miles from Cottonwood Wash Road, is a deep narrow canyon that makes for a good hike. The bridge over Bull Valley Gorge was first built in the 1940s but was not improved until after an auto accident in 1954. Three men died when their pickup truck stalled on the bridge and rolled into the gorge. The pickup can still be seen wedged into this narrow canyon.

After crossing Bull Valley Gorge, Skutumpah Road follows Indian Hollow up to a small pass. From the top of the pass the road straightens and improves, passing through the broad valleys of Bullrush Hollow and Lick Wash. This section of the road offers good views of the Pink Cliffs to the west and Table Mountain to the north. The White Cliffs come into view after passing Lick Wash.

Glendale Bench Road intersects Skutumpah Road about sixteen miles from Highway 89. Glendale Bench Road provides an alternate route to Highway 89, and Skutumpah Canyon Road continues down Johnson Canyon, cutting through the Vermilion Cliffs. The White Cliffs can often be seen to the north. Areas near the road in Johnson Canyon are mostly private property, but Long Canyon and Johnson Lakes Canyon are accessible.

Table Mountain

Eagle Gate Arch is located on the east side of the road three and a half miles before the junction with Highway 89. This is a fairly large arch and is one of the few freestanding arches in the monument. To see the arch, look for the sign indicating the "LDS Church Johnson Canyon Ranch." This sign is located on the west side of the road and is near one of the locations where the road crosses Johnson Wash. Drive south a few hundred feet from the sign and look carefully along the cliffs near the base of Johnson Canyon. The arch is located on a ridge between two side canyons.

Willis Creek (50)

Overview

Willis Creek is seldom visited, as most people prefer the more popular and dramatic Bull Valley Gorge. As it cuts through the White Cliffs, Willis Creek has a few sections of convoluted narrows that make good hiking. The creek flows year-round through the

Willis Creek

narrows, which is a good hike in the hot days of summer. Ponderosa pine trees grow along the canyon bottom and along the canyon walls.

Access

From Cottonwood Wash Road drive south six miles on Skutumpah Road to Willis Creek, which is easily spotted because it is one of the few canyons with running water. Sheep Creek is the only other wash in the area that has running water, and it is about three miles south of Cottonwood Wash Road. A large turnoff is present on the right side of the road just before crossing the creek. The trail starts where Willis Creek crosses the road. There is not much of a canyon near the road, but it is not long before Willis Creek enters into a deep and narrow canyon.

Difficulty

Hiking is easy down the relatively flat bottom of Willis Creek. Stream crossings are simple except for a few places in the narrows where the creek occupies the canyon's entire floor. At these spots, the water is only ankle deep and easily waded. It is two miles one way to the junction with Sheep Creek.

Maps

1:24,000 Bull Valley Gorge

Elevation

6,000 feet at trailhead with minimal loss/gain

Water

There is treatable water in Willis Creek.

Camping

An established campground exists at Kodachrome Basin State Park (31). Primitive car camping is found by taking a left at a pull-off just past Willis Creek. Backpackers can find a campsite along Sheep Creek.

Route Description

Once you leave the road, the canyon quickly narrows and deepens, cutting into the Navajo Sandstone of the White Cliffs. There are five short sections of narrows in the canyon between the road and Sheep Creek.

Averett Canyon enters Willis Creek on the left after three-quarters of a mile. You will pass a small arch in the main canyon just before Averett Canyon. It is possible to get back to the road via Averett Canyon, but a series of dry-falls must be negotiated. The easiest way around the dry-falls is on the left, but even this is difficult. This route back to the road via Averett Canyon is a little less than a mile. Averett Canyon is named after Elijah Averett, a Mormon from St. George who was killed by Indians in 1866 while leading an expedition to hunt down marauding Indians. A monument has been erected in his remembrance and is located about a hundred feet away from the left side of the wash. Look for an old trail halfway between the road and Willis Wash.

Willis Creek gradually becomes deeper and wider. There are only a few more very narrow sections below Averett Canyon. Large ponderosa pine trees grow in the fractured Navajo Sandstone and along the creek bottom. The canyon is quite deep when it enters Sheep Creek.

Sheep Creek has little or no water before Willis Creek enters. It is wider than Willis Canyon, but the fact that it cuts deep through the spectacular White Cliffs makes it a very scenic canyon. It is possible to follow Sheep Creek all the way down to its intersection with Bull Valley Gorge, about four miles, and then to hike out of Bull Valley Gorge, another five miles. This would make either a very long day hike or a two-day backpacking trip. Backpackers should bring a few sections of rope ten to fifteen feet in length to get their backpacks through the narrows of Bull Valley Gorge.

Bull Valley Gorge (51)

Overview

Bull Valley Gorge is one of the deepest and narrowest canyons in the monument. This picturesque canyon has a number of short sections of narrows and is filled with stately Douglas fir and ponderosa pine trees.

Access

Bull Valley Gorge is nine miles south of Cottonwood Wash Road. Willis Creek, which has a small stream, is crossed a mile and a half before arriving at Bull Valley Gorge. Park near the bridge going over the gorge.

Difficulty

Hikes in the canyon are fairly strenuous. The floor of the wash is quite rocky and uneven for the first three miles. Choke stones and dry-falls make the route even more challenging. Some upper-body strength is needed to overcome these obstacles. If you are not the strongest person, the hike is still possible, but it is necessary to bring along a partner. The first four miles of the canyon are the most narrow and scenic.

Map

1:24,000 Bull Valley Gorge

Elevation

Top: 6,050 feet
Bottom: 5,200 feet (at junction with Paria River)

Water

This narrow canyon has no running water.

Camping

Check out the established campground at Kodachrome Basin. There are also some possible car-camping sites near Willis Creek.

Route Description

Where the road crosses Bull Valley Gorge it is 150 feet deep and only ten to fifteen feet wide. The easiest way to enter the canyon is to walk three-quarters of a mile upstream from the bridge. A small trail can be followed upstream on the north side of the canyon along its rim. The canyon gradually becomes less deep until eventually it is easy to slip into its narrow confines. This walk above the canyon bottom provides an interesting perspective of the slot canyon. Among the vast landscape of juniper forests and flat-topped mesas the canyon is almost invisible to the eye, but as soon as it is entered it is like a window into a different realm.

Bull Valley Gorge

The canyon is easily entered, but the first obstacles are shortly encountered. Most of the difficult obstacles are between the entrance into the canyon and where it passes under the bridge. The first dry-fall and choke stones are difficult to get around. If you are by yourself, a rope will help lift a heavy pack.

Downstream, the bridge can be seen above you after about three-quarters of a mile. From here, the canyon narrows and widens a number of times. The deepest and narrowest sections of the canyon are about a half mile below the bridge. Walking gradually becomes easier as the canyon widens downstream.

A large number of Douglas fir trees grow in the cool and shaded confines of the canyon walls, and their beautiful green colors break up the metallic grey-and-tan colors of the Navajo Sandstone. Manzanita, with their distinctive waxy evergreen leaves, are also found in the canyon bottom.

Three miles downstream from the bridge the canyon makes a sharp turn to the east. No more narrows are present after this turn. The walking is easy in this part of the canyon and is a nice break after the rocky upper sections of the gorge. It is about five miles to the intersection with Sheep Creek. If you are interested in back-packing, you can head all the way down Sheep Creek to the Paria or you can hike to Skutumpah Road via Willis Creek.

Lick Wash (52)

Overview

Lick Wash is a narrow drainage that cuts through the White Cliffs. Giant pine trees grow in this sandy wash, and the creamy-colored cliffs of Navajo Sandstone are streaked with red desert varnish.

Access

Lick Wash crosses Skutumpah Road about eighteen miles south of where it left Cottonwood Wash Road. The road passes Willis Creek and Bull Valley Gorge before going over a small pass into a broad valley. Continue on through the valley, passing by a BLM sign for Bullrush Hollow, and then go over a rise into another broad valley through which Lick Wash runs down the middle. A flood advisory sign is posted where the wash crosses the road. This is the trailhead, and it is easy to park right after you cross the wash.

Difficulty

It is easy hiking down a desert wash, and it is also a nice place to escape the summer heat. Walking will be difficult right after a storm, as this wash bottom becomes particularly muddy. It is about three miles to Park Wash.

Maps

1:100,000 Kanab

1: 24,000 Deer Spring Point

Elevation

6,300 to 6,100 feet

Water

Water is only found in the wash during wet periods.

Camping

The best primitive car-camping sites are near Willis Creek (50).

Route Description

Before cutting through the White Cliffs, Lick Wash drains a broad basin. Follow the wash down from where you parked your car toward the tree-clad cliffs of Navajo Sandstone into a deep canyon.

Giant ponderosa pine trees and Douglas fir trees grow in the middle of Lick Wash. It seems as though these trees favor the narrowest parts of the canyon. Downstream the canyon gradually widens, but the tall sandstone cliffs persist on both sides. The canyon has three short sections of sandstone narrows.

No Mans Mesa, a large plateau, comes into view after about two miles. This mesa can be seen by looking straight down the canyon. The mesa is a pristine area; no animals have grazed here and no exotic species have been introduced.

The bright-red staining and desert varnish in the lower part of the wash is very pretty. A number of small side canyons come in before the canyon enters Park Wash. The canyon is very broad by the time it reaches Park Wash but still scenic.